What People Are Saying A[bout] John D. Barry and *Jesus' Ec[onomy]*

"In *Jesus' Economy*, John Barry points us toward a world where everyone has 'this day our daily bread.' Barry reminds us that God didn't make a world of scarcity, or a world with too many people. Poverty was created by you and me, as we fall short of loving our neighbors as ourselves. As Gandhi put it, 'There's enough for everyone's need, but not enough for everyone's greed.' We created poverty. And we can end it. Jesus and the early church show us the way. In this book, you will find an in-depth look at Scripture and economics and a beautiful vision for a world where everyone has enough."

—SHANE CLAIBORNE
Cofounder, The Simple Way and Red Letter Christians
Author, *The Irresistible Revolution* and *Common Prayer*

"*Jesus' Economy* is fast moving and 'heart' hitting. It will bring conviction. It will also give you hope. I am happy to commend its widest reading."

—DR. DANIEL L. AKIN
President, Southeastern Baptist Theological Seminary
Author or editor of numerous books and Bible commentaries, including *I Am Going* (with Bruce Riley Ashford) and *Vibrant Church* (with Thom S. Rainer)

"*Jesus' Economy* weaves together Scripture, realities of the world of poverty, and in-depth personal experience to produce a fine handbook for practical mission work. For John Barry, effective ministry is informed, holistic, and sacrificial—and his life bears this out."

—ROBERT D. LUPTON
Best-selling author of several books, including *Toxic Charity; Compassion, Justice, and the Christian Life;* and *Theirs Is the Kingdom*
President, FCS Urban Ministries

"We often think of poverty as just an economic issue, but poverty has both economic and spiritual roots and effects. John Barry understands this and in *Jesus' Economy*, he offers a long-term strategy for healing both physical and spiritual poverty: job creation, church planting, and meeting people's basic needs, with a focus on community development and sustainability."

—DR. JAY W. RICHARDS
Author of many books, including the *New York Times* best sellers
Infiltrated and *Indivisible*,
and the 2010 Templeton Enterprise Award-winner *Money, Greed, and God*
Research Assistant Professor, Busch School of Business, The Catholic University of America
Senior Fellow at Discovery Institute

"John Barry has written an inspiring and readable account about Jesus, poverty, and the mission of the church. This book tells you what poverty is, where it is, what Jesus said about it, and how you can follow Jesus' commands to end it. A great introduction to the socioeconomics of poverty, as well as Christian teaching on the subject. Great resource for pastors, students, and church groups!"

—REV. DR. MICHAEL F. BIRD
Author, *Evangelical Theology* and *What Christians Ought to Believe*
Academic Dean and Lecturer in Theology, Ridley College
Melbourne, Australia
Author, Euangelion blog, Patheos.com

"Considering the passion and action that John Barry and his wife, Kalene, have put into this project, I trust they must be prompted by God to do so. Barry shares deep insights into wealth and poverty from Jesus' perspective. *Jesus' Economy* is well worth reading, pondering, and putting into action, especially in this day and age."

—DR. JULIE LEE WU
President and Dean, China Bible Seminary, Hong Kong
Recipient of Women in Leadership Award from the Association of Theological Schools

"John Barry's *Jesus' Economy* is not just a must-read, but it is also a book that the global church needs to embrace and use to teach Jesus' life-changing and transformational principles. Barry is a terrific writer and an unusual type of Christian leader: he can correctly be described as a selfless, shepherd, servant type of leader. Barry's ministry, the nonprofit Jesus' Economy, makes a case for this book. *Jesus' Economy* is a narrative of how to conquer the twin enemies of the human race: corruption and poverty. Barry gives the church not just theories and empirical data on poverty, but also concrete and practical examples of Jesus and His disciples' models of poverty alleviation. Our churches in Africa can comfortably use this book in Sunday school or theological seminaries. I strongly recommend it to members of the global church who want to engage in the mission of God!"

—DR. SUNDAY BOBAI AGANG
Professor of Christian Ethics, Theology, and Public Policy
ECWA Theological Seminary, Kagoro, Nigeria
Fellow, Faculty of Theology, Stellenbosch University, South Africa
Author, *No More Cheeks to Turn?* and *When Evil Strikes: Faith and the Politics of Human Hostility*

"Jesus-followers with a kingdom perspective approach life as one big mission trip. John Barry's *Jesus' Economy* provides a clarion call to live as viral kingdom agents (the answer to 'Why am I here?') but also provides practical ways to love our neighbors ('What do I do?' and 'How do I do it?'). John accomplishes this without scolding and shaming. Instead, he persistently encourages. The message of the book is 'You can do this!' We sometimes allow difficult circumstances or stalled progress to challenge our faith in this certainty. Then a book like *Jesus' Economy* comes along and helps us believe all over again."

—DR. REGGIE MCNEAL
Best-selling author whose works include *The Present Future, Missional Renaissance, Kingdom Come, Kingdom Collaborators,* and *A Work of Heart*
Missional Leadership Specialist, Leadership Network

"Google 'your town name + poverty,' John Barry says, and you'll be surprised—not only by the problems but also by the resources you can tap into as you love your neighbors. In *Jesus' Economy*, Barry explains how the best practices include listening, affirming local assets, rooting work in churches on the ground, accountability, transparency, and tapping into specialized experts when they are needed. Whether our neighbors are global or local, whether they are unreached or undiscipled, whether they need the gospel or finance, they must be a priority for us because they are a priority for Jesus. This book shows how to make that happen, and how it is being done nearby and far away."

—DR. MIRIAM ADENEY
Associate Professor, Global and Urban Ministries, Seattle Pacific University
Board Member, *Christianity Today* International
Award-winning author, *Kingdom Without Borders: The Untold Story of Global Christianity*; *Daughters of Islam*; and *God's Foreign Policy*

"Although more people have been raised out of abject poverty in the last thirty years than ever before, in all of human history, there is still much work to be done. John Barry's new book, *Jesus' Economy: A Biblical View of Poverty, the Currency of Love, and a Pattern for Lasting Change*, gives us a practical, biblical, hands-on manual for loving and serving "the least of these." This book will not only change the way you look at poverty, it will help you find the role God is calling you to play in helping change the world."

—HUGH WHELCHEL
Executive Director, The Institute for Faith, Work & Economics
Author, *How Then Should We Work?*

"*Jesus' Economy* is a must-read for those concerned with the impoverished in our communities and in the world. John Barry believes that eliminating poverty should happen at both the physical and spiritual levels. His proposals are grounded in Scripture—providing great biblical insights on how to address poverty from God's perspective, affirming that Jesus is the key to overcoming poverty. *Jesus' Economy* is practical missional ministry at its best. I'm sure it will challenge you to go to the next level of a serious commitment to love your neighbor as yourself. I enthusiastically recommend it to everyone."

—REV. EDDY ALEMÁN
General Secretary, Reformed Church in America

"John D. Barry's new book, *Jesus' Economy*, is a bracing call for the church to be the church among the poor. You don't have to agree with every word... but you might. This book will thrill you, disturb you, and make you think. It may even cause you to make some changes in how you express your love for people who bear the same image you do."

—STAN GUTHRIE
Editor at Large, The Colson Center for Christian Worldview
Former Editor at Large, *Christianity Today*
Author, *Missions in the Third Millennium* and *All That Jesus Asks:*
How His Questions Can Teach and Transform Us

"You know all the crazy things Jesus said that we try to explain away? Commands like 'Deny yourself and take up your cross'? Or 'Sell your possessions and give the money to the poor'? Well, John Barry actually obeys them. And, I'm going to be honest: when I first started reading about his experience, I felt threatened. *What might Jesus be calling me to do?* But as I read about John's vision to eradicate poverty in Jesus' name—and about his dynamic interactions with needy people around the world—fear was replaced by hope. And then excitement. Jesus' Economy is a fantastic book that has inspired me to join John on God's mission of alleviating spiritual and physical poverty around the globe. Can you think of a greater mission?"

—DREW DYCK
Editor, CTPastors.com (a Christianity Today publication) and
Moody Publishers
Author, *Your Future Self Will Thank You*, *Yawning at Tigers*, and *Generation Ex-Christian*
Former Managing Editor, *Leadership Journal*

"Inspiring and eye-opening, John D . Barry's *Jesus' Economy* is a rallying cry for all believers to meditate on and rethink the Great Commission in practical, humanitarian terms. John and Kalene, as fellow humanitarians and followers of Jesus, are committed, as we are, to the cause of seeing poverty erased in our world through the only successful means possible—the way of Jesus Christ and His gospel."

—TASS SAADA
(author of the best-selling *Once an Arafat Man* and *The Mind of Terror*)
and **KAREN SAADA**
Founders, Hope for Ishmael, a reconciliation ministry between Arabs and Jews
Founders, Seeds of Hope, a humanitarian organization serving the people of Jerusalem,
Jericho, and Gaza

"*Jesus' Economy* is a powerful example of the application of principles we find in the influential Lausanne Covenant (1974), which contains a strong affirmation of faith in Christ and a renewed call to carry the complete gospel to the whole world. John Barry demonstrates, through engaging stories, persuasive exegesis, and personal testimony, that the mission of the church should be holistic. Christian leaders and practitioners will find this book a treasure trove of insight and encouragement."

—DR. CARLOS RAÚL SOSA SILIEZAR
Assistant Professor of New Testament, Wheaton College
Expert in Latin American Theology and the Gospels

"I don't believe I fully understood how the Bible views poverty until I read John Barry's book *Jesus' Economy*. John reminds us, with thoughtfulness and grace, that Christians must focus on the example of Jesus to address the problems of poverty in any relevant way. Filled with moving stories and compelling facts, *Jesus' Economy* examines a vague subject like poverty with great nuance, making it completely accessible and unendingly meaningful. *Jesus' Economy* gives us a poignant examination of an often-misunderstood topic. Don't ignore this important book."

—STEPHEN MCGARVEY
Vice President of Digital Content, Salem Web Network
Editor-in-chief, Crosswalk.com, Christianity.com, BibleStudyTools.com, iBelieve.com

"John Barry brings two breaths of fresh air to the study of a critical need in our world—alleviating poverty. First, he lives what he writes. *Jesus' Economy* did not rise from secondhand study. Instead, it blends solid research with real-life experience. Barry's writing represents the natural extension of his personal commitment in India and elsewhere. Second, he brings a decisively biblical answer to a problem addressed mostly by politics and finance. He exposes the folly of a government solution to a spiritual need. For believers and churches seeking better paths to changing this world, start the journey here."

—DR. GREG TRULL
Dean, School of Ministry and Director, Africa Training Partnership,
Corban University, Salem, OR

"I recommend *Jesus' Economy* to you and your church! Poverty statistics worldwide remain very high. Though Jesus told His disciples the poor would always be with them, such was not an excuse to neglect changing this global reality. Even the great missionary Paul, who preached the whole counsel of God, was eager to remember the poor in his ministry (Galatians 2:10). And we should too! John Barry has done a wonderful service in the kingdom of God by writing this book. *Jesus' Economy* will challenge and motivate you. But Barry does not leave you only with good thoughts; he offers many practical steps to bring about desperately needed change."

—DR. J. D. PAYNE
Author, *Discovering Church Planting, Apostolic Church Planting,*
and *Developing a Strategy for Missions*
Associate Professor of Christian Ministry, Samford University
Former National Missionary with North American Mission Board,
Southern Baptist Convention
Former Associate Professor of Church Planting and Evangelism and past director of the Center
for North American Missions and Church Planting, Southern Baptist Theological Seminary

"World Vision president emeritus Rich Stearns prolifically told all of us who are Christ followers about *The Hole in Our Gospel*. In *Jesus' Economy*, John Barry has now given us the motivation and instructions for why and how to fill in that vital missing part. He understands that a host of well-meaning people of faith have unintentionally prolonged the problem of poverty by offering short-term relief instead of long-term development and sustainability. By relating relevant Scripture and life experiences, Barry teaches us how to know the heart of Jesus and help desperate and destitute people experience total life transformation."

—JOHN ASHMEN
President, Citygate Network
(formerly The Association of Gospel Rescue Missions)
Author, *Invisible Neighbors*

"*Jesus' Economy* is about all of life as God intended it to be. Barry creatively articulates holistic living that transcends our varying theological persuasions and challenges us to embrace the sacrificial love of God as our motivation for service. This book bridges the gap between theory and practice, and provides principles that are applicable in multiple ministry contexts for lasting change. This is mandatory reading for all in Christian service!"

—DR. EMMANUEL BELLON
Vice President, Scholarleaders International
Author, *Leading Financial Sustainability in Theological Institutions*

"In Palestinian culture, we are accustomed to saying, 'If poverty were a man, I would have killed him.' This book shows us how Jesus wants to alleviate poverty through the sacrificial love of His followers. Such love is only possible through a vital relationship with Jesus and also with the poor. John D. Barry prophetically reminds us that we cannot be true followers of Jesus and ignore the poor. We cannot separate physical and spiritual poverty. In *Jesus' Economy*, we find disturbing contemporary data, heart-stirring stories, and inspiring challenges, as well as opportunities for ministry. The book informs us, inspires us, and gives us the opportunity to be involved in addressing poverty in biblical ways. I recommend this book to every Christian who desires to know how Jesus wants us to help the poor."

—REV. DR. YOHANNA KATANACHO
Academic Dean, Nazareth Evangelical College, Nazareth, Israel
Reconciliation leader in Israel
Author, *The Land of Christ: A Palestinian Cry*
Old Testament Editor, *Arabic Contemporary Commentary* and *Asia Bible Commentary*

"*Jesus' Economy* flows from the heart of God for the marginalized all over the world. Rooted in the nonprofit work of John and Kalene Barry, *Jesus' Economy* shows us not just how to effectively accomplish humanitarian and social goals, but how to minister to the poor. It's a vision of how to strengthen the work of the kingdom of God that John and his wife, Kalene, are living. This includes advice for church-planting movements, equipping leaders, health initiatives, and education. *Jesus' Economy* will help you achieve measurable transformation and develop people and communities."

—DR. ERIC COSTANZO
Senior Pastor, South Tulsa Baptist Church
Author, *Harbor for the Poor*

"*Jesus' Economy* is an invitation to a journey of faith in Christ's transformative love. It equips you to uplift and to dignify the poor and, in so doing, glorifies Jesus Christ, who became poor that the world may experience the riches of that transformative love. The book also challenges humanity, particularly the church, to live a life of fruitfulness and worthy sacrifice."

—DR. DAVID K. NGARUIYA
Director of PhD in Theological Studies Program and
Associate Professor of Intercultural Studies
Nairobi International School of Theology/International Leadership University
Nairobi, Kenya
Coeditor, *Communities of Faith in Africa and the African Diaspora*

"Jesus' Economy offers a sound biblical understanding of poverty—both its roots and its alleviation. John's text is personal and sincere, written with humility, and reflects the author's actual experience of dealing with the needy. The approach he advocates is relational and holistic, bringing the soul and the body together. Moreover, John offers some very practical and feasible ideas of how to alleviate poverty through the local church. Worth reading!"

—DR. ANDREY KRAVTSEV
President of Intercultural Connections
(a nonprofit organization in Russia that mobilizes pastors and others
to serve in areas with little Christian presence)
Former President, North Caucasus Bible Institute of Russia

"Jesus' Economy is a wonderful biblical and practical study—and it comes from the heart and mind of an expert in the field. John Barry sheds light on one of the most important issues of our day: that the church recognize its mission, not only inside its walls, but also outside them—looking after the impoverished, those whom Jesus cared about the most. The only hope for overcoming poverty in the world today is in Jesus and His church. Please don't read this book if you are not ready to change your heart, mind, and attitude!"

—REV. DR. THARWAT WAHBA
Chairman, Missions Department, Evangelical Theological Seminary
Cairo, Egypt
Chairman of Council, Pastoral and Outreach Ministries for the Evangelical (Presbyterian)
Church of Egypt
Author, *The Practice of Mission in Egypt*

"Jesus' Economy provides a fresh and compelling examination of Jesus' teachings about poverty and the poor. Both personal and practical, it is a must-read for those who are tired of lukewarm and incomplete Christian endeavor to help those facing desperate economic challenges. It renews hope in the power of Jesus' love to genuinely transform lives and communities—including our own!"

—SYLVIA FOTH
Founder and President Emeritus, Kidzana Ministries
(a nonprofit equipping children's workers and leaders around the world)

"The title *Jesus' Economy: A Biblical View of Poverty, the Currency of Love, and a Pattern for Lasting Change* is an incredible description of what you will discover in John Barry's new book. It is an excellent resource on the life and ministry of Jesus Christ as a model for the contemporary church. Reading *Jesus' Economy* will provide you with a foundation for holistic, cross-cultural ministry in a world void of love and compassion. The church is called to be part of God's transforming mission to bring His kingdom to all nations. Barry shows how we can empower the global church by supporting the work of indigenous leaders and local believers. I heartily recommend this book to all who want to gain a biblical and theological perspective on how to follow and model Jesus today."

—DR. ANTONIO CARLOS BARRO
Founder and CEO, South American Theological Seminary
Londrina, Brazil

"What can we do to bring about restoration and transformation in our society, which is in many ways characterized by injustice, unfairness, and brokenness? First, we need a new outlook and a new approach. *Jesus' Economy* will not only change your perspective of the world but also motivate you to change your response toward those who are suffering and impoverished. John Barry discusses the stark reality of society's brokenness, including the unjust distribution of resources in the world. But he also provides a framework for creating a better world as we join hands with Christ, who died to transform society holistically. *Jesus' Economy* is a great resource for any context."

—DR. A. N. LAL SENANAYAKE
President, Lanka Bible College and Seminary
Peradeniya, Sri Lanka
Coeditor, *Educating for Tomorrow: Theological Leadership for the Asian Context*

"*Jesus' Economy* is a clear demonstration of the good news in action! John Barry shows us how God's powerful grace and cross-shaped love are being manifested in our world of dire need. With moving stories, engaging information, and relevant teaching about empowering the impoverished and sharing the gospel, we are given a front-row seat to many such godly interventions. Barry, who is eminently competent to lead us on an incredible journey, shows us how we, too, can partner in nothing less than 'Jesus' economy.'"

—DR. JACOB CHERIAN
Vice President and Dean of Faculty, Southern Asia Bible College
Kothanur, Bangalore, India

"*Jesus' Economy* is both a significant scholarly effort and a practical manual for missions. It reaches the North American reader, as well as my context of Eastern Europe and other regions. John Barry challenges, on both biblical (special revelation) and logical (general revelation) terms, the American church's contemporary perspective on global missions. He invites us to work toward a holistic approach of sharing the gospel. We do this by moving away from both the culturally insensitive, imperialistic paradigm and the culturally sensitive, 'withdrawal' method—which prevents the contemporary church from achieving its global impact. *Jesus' Economy* demonstrates how we can serve and empower the impoverished by allowing indigenous leaders to lead the way while providing for basic needs, fully loving other people, and giving sacrificially."

—DR. GELU PAUL-FAINA
Founding pastor, Vox Domini Baptist (Multisite) Church, Romania
President and founder, Churches with Global Impact
National Director, Ambassadors for Christ Romania

"Oriented in the global landscape of poverty and impoverishment, John D. Barry's *Jesus' Economy* is biblically anchored and remarkably personal. His self-engaged 'I-voice' and narrative approach will appeal to audiences of all ages—'to all who hope to make the world a better place.' Captivating both in theme and writing style, *Jesus' Economy* is a delightful read—informative and thought-provoking yet practical, providing pointers and directives for alleviating poverty both overseas and right where you live."

—DR. BARBARA M. LEUNG LAI
Research Professor of Old Testament, Tyndale University College & Seminary
Toronto, ON, Canada
International trainer of missionaries
Author, *Glimpsing the Mystery: The Book of Daniel*

"In *Jesus' Economy*, with the passion that characterizes him, John Barry challenges us to revisit our commitment to the needy, from two fronts. First, through a compelling case, he invites us to study and follow Jesus' dedication to the poor. Second, due to his broad experience in the field, he gives invaluable advice to those who are involved in—or looking to be involved in—ministries to the impoverished around the world."

—DR. NELSON MORALES
Professor of New Testament Studies, Seminario Teológico Centroamericano
Guatemala

"In *Jesus' Economy*, John Barry presents two major theses: first, we cannot separate spiritual poverty and material poverty; second, the only way to solve the problem of poverty at its root is love. The first thesis implies that the people of God are uniquely equipped to help the poor of the world. The second thesis may sound a bit simplistic, but Barry gives ample examples that helping the poor must begin with a genuine personal relationship with those in need. Only love can empower the poor to stand on their own. Without genuine relationship, our works of charity may actually hurt the ones we want to help. The book also gives an interesting exegesis of Paul's view on poverty, and offers much practical advice on how to help needy people in our communities. This book is written by someone with lots of experience in fighting poverty in the real world, and is a great manual for those who intend to fight poverty in their own neighborhood."

—KIN YIP LOUIE
Associate Professor, China Graduate School of Theology, Hong Kong
Author, *The Beauty of the Triune God*

"*Jesus' Economy* presents a powerful opportunity to bring about change in a broken world. I thank God for brave people like John Barry who follow God's calling on His great mission. This book is about changing our mind-set on how best to alleviate poverty—moving from a segmented approach to a holistic one. To create an understanding of the depth of the needs we are dealing with, Barry cites a number of the UN's Sustainable Development Goals and 'fast facts,' under such aims as 'No Poverty,' 'Zero Hunger,' and 'Quality Education.' Then Barry challenges us to lift the impoverished using Jesus' economy (self-sacrifice) and His currency (love). This book is both Scripture-based and mindful of the reality of poverty today. It is a passionate appeal that seeks to ignite hope for progress, inspire a commitment to empower people entrenched in poverty, and offer practical ways to transform lives."

—DR. SEBLEWONGEL ASRAT DENNEQUE
Holistic Child Development department head and faculty member
Evangelical Theological College
Addis Ababa, Ethiopia

"*Jesus' Economy* is an honest, powerful, fact-based analysis of the reality of poverty in our times. It is also a strong, biblically grounded, pragmatic proposal for addressing the issue of poverty by the Christian community. What John Barry defines as 'Jesus' economy' is a contemporary proposal for the extension of the kingdom's most basic principles into contemporary, and mainly secular, cultures. Barry makes a persuasive theological case for active Christian involvement in response to poverty. A must-read for those who long for authentic 'Your kingdom come' transformation in our neighborhoods and nations."

—DR. DARIUSZ DAREK JARMOLA
Founder, Go Global Ltd.
Former Vice President and Director of Global Studies, Oklahoma Wesleyan University
Past organizer and leader of humanitarian projects for various NGOs in Asia, Africa,
Latin America, and Europe

"*Jesus' Economy*...what a revelation! John Barry has nailed it. We have been full-time missionaries living and serving in Haiti for twenty-seven years, and we wish this book had been written when we first moved here. It would have saved us many heartaches and steered us in the right direction to help the poor. In poverty-stricken countries and areas, our hearts tell us to 'give people a fish to eat' as soon as possible. But this is not the whole answer. The answer is teaching them about Jesus, the great Fisherman, and then 'teaching them how to fish,' to earn their living. We call this 'food for life.' They must all have Jesus, but they must also be given the dignity of having a job and depending on the Lord to help and guide them. This is the answer to world hunger and poverty. Awesome!"

—BOBBY AND SHERRY BURNETTE
Founders and Directors, Love a Child, Inc.
Coauthors, *Love Is Something You Do*

"In the context of the developing world, *Jesus' Economy* translates the Scriptures into reality. John Barry shows that we must first live *within* the sacred text—allowing it to read us, examine us, bring life to us, and transform us. It is here where we personally encounter God. In this way, with the biblical text as our interpretive lens, drawing us into communion with God, we can understand how to best eradicate poverty according to Jesus' economy of sacrifice and love."

—BISHOP PHILIPO MAFUJA MAGWANO
Africa Inland Church, Tanzania

"John Barry's *Jesus' Economy* is a must-read for anyone who wants to make the world a better place by empowering the impoverished. Barry not only explains the issues of poverty, but he also offers long-term solutions for its alleviation, particularly in the developing world. He argues that lifting the impoverished requires addressing their spiritual needs as well as their physical ones. It also requires a sustainable system of 'creating jobs, planting churches, meeting basic needs, and training people.' For Barry, such assistance is motivated by Jesus' 'currency of love.' *Jesus' Economy* has given me fresh ideas about what it means to help others, and will change my giving habits."

—DR. XIAXIA E. XUE
Assistant Professor of New Testament Studies, China Graduate School of Theology, Hong Kong
Author, *Paul's Viewpoint on God, Israel, and the Gentiles in Romans 9–11*

JESUS'
ECONOMY

JESUS' ECONOMY

A BIBLICAL VIEW OF POVERTY, THE CURRENCY OF LOVE, AND A PATTERN FOR LASTING CHANGE

JOHN D. BARRY

WHITAKER
HOUSE

JESUS' ECONOMY:
A Biblical View of Poverty, the Currency of Love, and a Pattern for Lasting Change

John D. Barry
www.JesusEconomy.org
info@jesuseconomy.org
1-855-355-3266

ISBN: 978-1-64123-175-6
eBook ISBN: 978-1-64123-176-3
Printed in the United States of America
© 2019 by John D. Barry

Whitaker House
1030 Hunt Valley Circle
New Kensington, PA 15068
www.whitakerhouse.com

Library of Congress Cataloging-in-Publication Data (pending)

1 2 3 4 5 6 7 8 9 10 11 ⦿ 26 25 24 23 22 21 20 19

100% of author's proceeds go to the nonprofit Jesus' Economy, to fuel the movement of creating jobs and churches in the developing world.

Creating jobs and churches

www.jesuseconomy.org

1-855-355-3266

Jesus' Economy is an innovative 501(c)(3) non-profit, founded in 2012. We believe that eliminating poverty in our world should happen at both the physical and spiritual level. That's why we create holistic change in every partner community by simultaneously creating jobs, planting churches, and meeting basic needs. On JesusEconomy.org, you can shop fair trade from hundreds of artisans around the world, and give to the cause of your choice, such as church planting, empowering women, or providing clean water. 100% of your giving goes directly to your cause, every time.

Join the movement at JesusEconomy.org

To all who hope to make the world a better place.

CONTENTS

PROLOGUE

Opportunities like never before.

PART ONE

*The problem of poverty. How our world works.
And envisioning a better reality.*

PART TWO

*God's view of the impoverished. What the Bible says about poverty.
And what that really means.*

PART THREE

*The myths of poverty. What followers of Jesus should say in response.
And really understanding poverty.*

PART FOUR

Some very practical ideas for overcoming poverty.
How you can truly love people. And why it won't be easy.

EPILOGUE

Never stop truly loving.

PROLOGUE: OPPORTUNITIES LIKE NEVER BEFORE

Jesus' economy is based on self-sacrifice. Jesus' currency is love.

This idea changed my entire life.

● ● ●

In 2012, my wife, Kalene, and I founded the international nonprofit Jesus' Economy, dedicated to creating jobs and churches in the developing world. While we were studying the theory behind economic development strategies and spreading the vision to others, we felt God calling us to a deeper understanding of truly *living* the message. After years of prayer, we sold our house and nearly everything we owned, dedicating ourselves fully to spreading the gospel and alleviating poverty.

My story isn't unique. Each of us is called, in some way, to an equally radical life change: to complete mental and spiritual transformation in Christ. According to Paul the apostle, we are to "die to self" and put on our new selves in the likeness of God. (See Ephesians 4:17–31.)

This book is about living your story of self-sacrifice for the sake of the poor and hurting in the world and those yet to hear the name of Jesus. It is about renewing our lives in Christ.

● ● ●

All over the world, even in our own neighborhoods, there are people in need, both physically and spiritually. Jesus wants us to be a part of changing this reality. But *how* can we do that?

It was while sitting in front of theological books and the biblical text in its original languages that I gained a head-knowledge of the answers. But it was while working with the impoverished that I realized what those answers *really* meant.

The stories in this book do not come from full-time ministry. While writing this book, I had a full-time job as a chief editor and publisher for Logos Bible Software (now Faithlife Corporation), overseeing their original content publishing efforts. I was practicing ministry on the side of my day gig: as a chapel minister and treasurer for a homeless rescue shelter, as the president of a church plant, and eventually as the CEO and founder of the nonprofit Jesus' Economy. That's why I know the methods in this book are for all of us, no matter our vocation or calling. I have seen people transform lives at kitchen tables, in hospitals, on the street, in remote villages, on the Internet, in government offices, and anywhere else God has called them to be. We are missionaries wherever we are, no matter our title.

And while I certainly haven't "arrived" spiritually, following Jesus into the unknown has meant everything to me. I want you to experience the wonder and blessing of following Jesus in a similar way. I want you to experience the authentic and biblical Jesus who is deeply challenging. I want you to meet the Jesus who calls us to live as part of an entirely different economy, one based on self-sacrifice.

Jesus gave up His life so that we can be resurrected with Him. Now, He calls us to do the same: give of ourselves for the impoverished, the marginalized, and the outsider; spread His message of love, freedom from sin, and the power to live a better life.

It is through God's leading that we are able to accomplish this work.

God provides the resources we need to bring the gospel to the world, through the power of the Holy Spirit and the gifts He gives. This means that all of our resources, time, and energy are ultimately a gift from God—a gift to be shared with others.

● ● ●

I wrote this book because, as a publisher and as a minister, I saw a gap in the theology of poverty alleviation. I realized that the average

American doesn't know what the Bible *really* says about poverty—or how Jesus approached it—and furthermore doesn't know how to actually go about alleviating poverty in their own lives and in the lives of others.

If you desire to show true compassion to the impoverished—and are ready to realize the ways you are impoverished too—this book is for you. If you want to see Jesus completely revolutionize the way you approach loving Him and others, this book is for you. If you want to see every last person on the planet experience the power of the resurrected Christ in every part of their life, you're about to learn how—and it starts with you.

Faith in action is what it is all about. No matter what your cultural background or context, Jesus' economy has implications for you. While the practical advice I offer has in view my particular context of the United States and Canada, the pattern I propose is intended to be applicable globally. This global application has been confirmed by Christian leaders from nearly every continent who have graciously read this book and suggested it be utilized in their contexts.

Join me and other Christians around the globe in learning to live Jesus' economy. Together in Christ, we can transform our world.

PART ONE

The problem of poverty. How our world works.
And envisioning a better reality.

YELLOW PAPER CROWNS

In a remote village in Bihar, India, I sat in a room surrounded by children wearing yellow paper crowns. They were princes and princesses in God's kingdom, according to the missionaries who were speaking that day.

I sat in the corner and tried to imagine what these kids were thinking. How could they believe that they were *chosen* or *royalty*, that they were truly loved by God, when the rest of their world told them a different narrative?

They were going home to brick-and-mud houses with dung stuck on the wall to dry and be used for fuel. They had been abandoned by their own government—left without clean water until a partner organization of the nonprofit Jesus' Economy drilled a well for their village. Some had been orphaned by parents who were forced to go elsewhere for work. Yet here they were, hearing the name of Jesus for the very first time and fully accepting that they were created in the image of God. That God *loved* and *chose* them. (See Genesis 1:26–27; John 3:16; Ephesians 1:4–5.)

In that moment, a sense of responsibility overwhelmed me. I realized that loving these children and their families meant not just giving them *part* of the good news of Jesus, but *all of it*—full spiritual and physical renewal. I could no longer just address their physical poverty through aid and relief or just their spiritual poverty through preaching the gospel. The two are intimately connected and must work together to bring about real change.

It took me years of training—studying how Jesus looks at the world—to begin to understand how to accomplish this. It's a learning process I'm still in (and always will be). As a Christian, you never really arrive. You're always in process, constantly learning to live by the terms of the living God. Yet, through Christ, we can accomplish everything He calls us to do.

In Bihar, there are over 101 million people who have *never* heard the name of Jesus—a practically unreached people group. But through the meeting of physical *and* spiritual needs, together as one *holistic* plan, things are changing.

I met a man in Bihar who had lived his entire life as a gang leader. An indigenous church planter had a chance encounter with him and shared about the freedom and love of Jesus. The gang leader was intrigued. His life felt so dark and empty, and local religion couldn't offer any hope for what he was feeling and experiencing. Before long, he decided to believe in Jesus. It changed his entire life. He went out into a field and buried his gun and knife. He dedicated his life to co-laboring for Jesus—working manual labor and spreading the word about Jesus whenever possible.

This story reminds me of Isaiah 2:4:

[God] shall judge between the nations, and shall decide disputes for many peoples; and they shall beat their swords into plowshares, and their spears into pruning hooks; nation shall not lift up sword against nation, neither shall they learn war anymore. (ESV)

This is the power and liberty of the gospel that is going forth around the world. Will you join in the movement?

WHAT DOES A BETTER WORLD LOOK LIKE TO YOU?

What does a better world look like to you? Truly loving people starts with prayer and discernment—learning what a better world looks like to God.

Seeing things from God's perspective is a *process*. It is the process of imagining what isn't yet, but should be. When the author of Hebrews describes faith, this sort of language is used: "Now faith is the assurance of *things hoped for*, the conviction of things not seen" (Hebrews 11:1 ESV). Hope itself rests firmly on what Jesus *has* accomplished and *will accomplish* in our world. This hope, when coupled with compassion and generosity, will produce true change.

If the future actually could look different than the trajectory humanity is currently on, what would you want it to look like?

I desire to see poverty alleviated, so that people can live freely and with purpose—so that they can accomplish good for others in the world. I long for Jesus to become a major part of people's lives, because I know the difference He has made in my life and the lives of others. I want to watch transformation in Christ. I want to see entire communities renewed.

I believe that we have the opportunities and capabilities today to make this happen. I believe that Christ has given us—all of humanity—the great gift of renewal through Him. We can roll out a strategy for community development that doesn't change just *one part* of a person's life, but their *whole* life. We, collectively, can overcome spiritual and physical poverty.

Because...Hope Is Miraculous

The developing world is full of people with tenacity and strength who lack the resources to make their dreams reality. They need hope and someone to empower them to realize their dreams (and to dream with them). They need to see peace brought to their communities and to experience faith that can overcome adversity.

The incredible thing about offering someone hope is that doing so also offers you hope. It makes you believe in what the person you're empowering has yet to see. It changes the way you feel about the state of that person's life and causes you to think about what hope God has in store for you. It gives you a small glimpse of God's eternal perspective—you briefly see the connections He does: how He has used you to help someone else, and how He will likely use someone else to help you.

When we give of our time, money, or resources, we have the opportunity to watch Jesus' work in the world.

I believe that Jesus—as the hope spoken of in Hebrews 11:1—has great opportunities in store for our generation. It is His work through the Spirit that the whole world is anticipating, whether we realize it or not.

Because...Jesus Is Working Even Now

It is Jesus' second coming that we wait for. But it is His work *now* that we live for. As Christians, we are convicted that Jesus was resurrected from death and is working even today. Sadly, many people wait a lifetime for the right opportunity to partner with Him.

God is presenting us with life-changing opportunities right now. If we will simply look around, we will see them. If we will pray earnestly, we will recognize how awesome God is and how much work He is doing at this very moment.

God wants to use you for great things. Today is the day you can bring hope to those in need. Today is the day you can acknowledge that hope is something all people deserve. Hope is something we can bring to others in the name of Jesus—it ignites the power to dream.

What does a better world look like to you? What will you do to make your vision for a better world a reality?

SPIRITUAL AND PHYSICAL POVERTY—IT'S ALL CONNECTED

Poverty is the outward symptom of a condition that has spread in societies throughout time. It might have been inflicted on you, or you might be a perpetrator of it, but the root cause is still the same: distance from God and His plan for our world.

The further we distance ourselves from God, the more we *forget*. We forget compassion for humanity. We forget to look out for others in addition to ourselves. We forget how broken we truly are. And it all began on the day sin entered the world and our relationship with God, the source of abundance and life, was broken. (See Genesis 3.)

Our physical poverty is easiest to observe: a lack of jobs, a lack of basic needs being met, corrupt and unstable societies, violence, a lack of access to education, women being viewed as lower than men, and similar maladies.

Our spiritual poverty is equally observable yet rarely addressed outside of Christian circles. Think of the Lord's Prayer, which we often recite in church, and which is based on Matthew 6 and Luke 11. Here's a close translation to the original Greek of Matthew 6:12: "Forgive us our *debts*, as we also forgive *our debtors*." The Greek of Luke 11:4 renders the same line this way: "Forgive us *our sins*, for also we ourselves forgive anyone *indebted* to us." Now think of a few common renderings of the Lord's Prayer: "Forgive us our *sins*, as we forgive those who have *sinned against us*," or "Forgive us our *trespasses*, as we forgive those who have *trespassed against us*." We naturally see the wrongs inside ourselves as a type of spiritual debt. It's spiritual poverty. And only Jesus can make that right.

This is why Paul says:

And you, who were dead in your trespasses…, God made alive together with him, having forgiven us all our trespasses, by canceling the record of debt that stood against us with its legal demands. This he set aside, nailing it to the cross.

(Colossians 2:13–14 esv)

The debt we owe, Jesus has paid. On the cross, our spiritual debt has been forgiven.

Yet, we all know that we continue to do wrong against God and other people. We all know that there are parts of us that have not been fully transformed by God. This is our ongoing spiritual poverty that still needs to change. The biblical vision is that we would be open to God working in us, allowing Him to transform us.

The realization of our own spiritual and physical poverty should give us deep compassion for those who live both without the knowledge of Jesus and without the means for sustainable survival. While we can never hope to fully solve these problems until Christ returns (see, for example, Matthew 26:11), we must dedicate ourselves to the work until He comes.

POVERTY BY THE NUMBERS: THE SUSTAINABLE DEVELOPMENT GOALS

Maybe you're not a data person—that's okay—but I provide the following information so that we can all have a little perspective about the problem, as well as the positive change that could be!

On September 25, 2015, leaders from the United Nations and from countries around the world got together to adopt the "Sustainable Development Goals." The seventeen goals are designed to address physical poverty, environmental protection, prosperity, and equality for all people. A fifteen-year plan was set in motion at that conference, so that by 2030, hopefully all the goals will be met. But it's not just governments and nonprofits doing the work. We—the neighbors, parents, employees, employers, students, travelers, and children of the world—are called to do our part as well.

> For the goals to be reached, everyone needs to do their part: governments, the private sector, civil society and people like you.
>
> —United Nations

The 2030 Sustainable Development Goals are as follows:

1. No Poverty

2. Zero Hunger

3. Good Health and Well-Being

4. Quality Education

5. Gender Equality

6. Clean Water and Sanitation

7. Affordable and Clean Energy

8. Decent Work and Economic Growth

9. Industry, Innovation and Infrastructure

10. Reduce Inequalities

11. Sustainable Cities and Communities

12. Responsible Production and Consumption

13. Climate Action

14. Life Below Water

15. Life on Land

16. Peace, Justice and Strong Institutions

17. Partnerships for the Goals

We will be dealing directly with a few of the goal topics in this book. Because of this, I've included a brief description of the goals we reference and some "fast facts" for you to keep in mind as you read.[1]

No Poverty

"Extreme poverty rates have been cut by more than half since 1990. While this is a remarkable achievement, one in five people in developing regions still live on less than $1.90 a day [USD], and there are millions more who make little more than this daily amount, plus many people risk slipping back into poverty.

"Poverty is more than the lack of income and resources to ensure a sustainable livelihood. Its manifestations include hunger and malnutrition, limited access to education and other basic services, social discrimination and exclusion as well as the lack

---

1. The above quoted material, as well as the majority of the following quotes and "Fast Facts," are from "Sustainable Development Goals: 17 Goals to Transform Our World," © 2018 United Nations, www.UN.org/sustainabledevelopment (accessed between May 22, 2018 and June 10, 2018). Reprinted with the permission of the United Nations. Some spelling has been changed to American usage and currencies have been clarified.

of participation in decision-making. Economic growth must be inclusive to provide sustainable jobs and promote equality."

Fast Facts:

- 767 million people live below the international poverty line of $1.90 a day [USD].

- In 2016, almost 10 percent of the world's workers live with their families on less than $1.90 per person per day.

- The overwhelming majority of people living below the poverty line belong to two regions: Southern Asia and sub-Saharan Africa. High poverty rates are often found in small, fragile and conflict-affected countries.

- Every day in 2014, 42,000 people had to abandon their homes to seek protection due to conflict.

Zero Hunger

"It is time to rethink how we grow, share and consume our food.

"If done right, agriculture, forestry and fisheries can provide nutritious food for all and generate decent incomes, while supporting people-centred rural development and protecting the environment.

"Climate change is putting even more pressure on the resources we depend on, increasing risks associated with droughts and floods. Many rural women and men can no longer make ends meet on their land, forcing them to migrate to cities in search of opportunities.

"A profound change of the global food and agriculture system is needed if we are to nourish today's 815 million hungry and the additional 2 billion people expected by 2050.

"The food and agriculture sector offers key solutions for development, and is central for hunger and poverty eradication."

Fast Facts:

+ Globally, one in nine people in the world today (815 million) are undernourished.

+ The vast majority of the world's hungry people live in developing countries, where 12.9 percent of the population is undernourished.

+ Poor nutrition causes nearly half (45 percent) of deaths in children under five—3.1 million children each year.

+ One in four of the world's children suffer stunted growth. In developing countries the proportion can rise to one in three.

+ 66 million primary school-age children attend classes hungry across the developing world, with 23 million in Africa alone.

+ Agriculture is the single largest employer in the world, providing livelihoods for 40 percent of today's global population. It is the largest source of income and jobs for poor rural households.

+ 500 million small farms worldwide, most still rainfed, provide up to 80 percent of food consumed in a large part of the developing world. Investing in smallholder women and men is an important way to increase food security and nutrition for the poorest, as well as food production for local and global markets.

+ If women farmers had the same access to resources as men, the number of hungry in the world could be reduced by up to 150 million.

Good Health and Well-Being

"Ensuring healthy lives and promoting the well-being for all at all ages is essential to sustainable development. Significant strides have been made in increasing life expectancy and reducing some of the common killers associated with child and maternal mortality. Major progress has been made on increasing access to clean water and sanitation, [and] reducing malaria, tuberculosis, polio and the spread of HIV/AIDS. However, many more efforts are needed to fully eradicate a wide range of diseases and address many different persistent and emerging health issues."

Fast Facts:

- 17,000 fewer children die each day than in 1990, but more than six million children still die before their fifth birthday each year.

- Children born into poverty are almost twice as likely to die before the age of five as those from wealthier families.

- Children of educated mothers—even mothers with only primary schooling—are more likely to survive than children of mothers with no education.

- Maternal mortality has fallen by almost 50 percent since 1990. But maternal mortality ratio—the proportion of mothers that do not survive childbirth compared to those who do—in developing regions is still 14 times higher than in the developed regions. Only half of women in developing regions receive the recommended amount of health care they need.

- AIDS is now the leading cause of death among adolescents (aged 10–19) in Africa and the second most common cause of death among adolescents globally.

Quality Education

"Obtaining a quality education is the foundation to improving people's lives and sustainable development. Major progress has been made towards increasing access to education at all levels and increasing enrollment rates in schools particularly for women and girls. Basic literacy skills have improved tremendously, yet bolder efforts are needed to make even greater strides for achieving universal education goals. For example, the world has achieved equality in primary education between girls and boys, but few countries have achieved that target at all levels of education."

Fast Facts:

+ Enrollment in primary education in developing countries has reached 91 percent but 57 million children remain out of school. More than half of children that have not enrolled in school live in sub-Saharan Africa.

+ An estimated 50 percent of out-of-school children of primary school age live in conflict-affected areas.

+ 103 million youth worldwide lack basic literacy skills, and more than 60 percent of them are female.

Gender Equality

"Women and girls continue to suffer discrimination and violence in every part of the world.

"Gender equality is not only a fundamental human right, but a necessary foundation for a peaceful, prosperous and sustainable world.

"Providing women and girls with equal access to education, health care, decent work, and representation in political and economic decision-making processes will fuel sustainable economies and benefit societies and humanity at large."

Fast Facts (this time from the World Bank):[2]

+ It is estimated that if women earned as much as men, they would add an additional $160 trillion in human capital worldwide (for the 141 countries included in the analysis).

---

2. "Unrealized Potential: The High Cost of Gender Inequality in Earnings," May 30, 2018, https://www.worldbank.org/en/topic/gender/publication/unrealized-potential-the-high-cost-of-gender-inequality-in-earnings.

- In many countries, girls' average educational attainment remains lower than boys, and adult women are less literate than men. Apart from these gender gaps in educational attainment, discrimination and social norms shape the terms of female labor force participation. Women are less likely than men to join the labor force and to work for pay. When they do, they are more likely to work part-time, in the informal sector, or in occupations that have lower pay. These disadvantages translate into substantial gender gaps in earnings, which in turn decrease women's bargaining power and voice.

Clean Water and Sanitation

"There is sufficient fresh water on the planet to achieve clean, accessible water for all. But due to bad economics or poor infrastructure, every year millions of people, most of them children, die from diseases associated with inadequate water supply, sanitation and hygiene.

"Water scarcity, poor water quality and inadequate sanitation negatively impact food security, livelihood choices and educational opportunities for poor families across the world. Drought afflicts some of the world's poorest countries, worsening hunger and malnutrition.

"By 2050, at least one in four people is likely to live in a country affected by chronic or recurring shortages of fresh water."

Fast Facts:

- 2.6 billion people have gained access to improved drinking water sources since 1990, but 663 million people are still without.
- At least 1.8 billion people globally use a source of drinking water that is fecally contaminated.

+ Between 1990 and 2015, the proportion of the global population using an improved drinking water source has increased from 76 percent to 91 percent. But water scarcity affects more than 40 percent of the global population and is projected to rise.

+ 2.4 billion people lack access to basic sanitation services, such as toilets or latrines.

+ Each day, nearly 1,000 children die due to preventable water and sanitation-related diarrhoeal diseases.

Decent Work and Economic Growth

"A continued lack of decent work opportunities, insufficient investments and under-consumption lead to an erosion of the basic social contract underlying democratic societies: that all must share in progress.

"Sustainable economic growth will require societies to create the conditions that allow people to have quality jobs that stimulate the economy while not harming the environment. Job opportunities and decent working conditions are also required for the whole working age population."

Fast Facts:

+ Global unemployment increased from 170 million in 2007 to nearly 202 million in 2012, of which about 75 million are young women and men.

+ Nearly 2.2 billion people live below the $2 per day [USD] poverty line; poverty eradication is only possible through stable and well-paid jobs.

+ 470 million jobs are needed globally for new entrants to the labor market between 2016 and 2030.

Industry, Innovation and Infrastructure

"Investments in infrastructure—transport, irrigation, energy and information and communication technology—are crucial to achieving sustainable development and empowering communities in many countries. It has long been recognized that growth in productivity and incomes, and improvements in health and education outcomes require investment in infrastructure."

Fast Facts:

- Basic infrastructure like roads, information and communication technologies, sanitation, electrical power and water remains scarce in many developing countries.

- About 2.6 billion people in the developing world are facing difficulties in accessing electricity full time.

- 1–1.5 billion people do not have access to reliable phone services.

- Inadequate infrastructure leads to a lack of access to markets, jobs, information and training, creating a major barrier to doing business.

- Undeveloped infrastructures limit access to health care and education.

- Small and medium-sized enterprises that engage in industrial processing and manufacturing are the most critical for the early stages of industrialization and are typically the largest job creators. They make up over 90 percent of business worldwide and account for between 50–60 percent of employment.

Peace, Justice, and Strong Institutions

"Goal 16 of the Sustainable Development Goals is dedicated to the promotion of peaceful and inclusive societies for sustainable development, the provision of access to justice for all, and building effective, accountable institutions at all levels."

Fast Facts:

- Among the institutions most affected by corruption are the judiciary and police.
- Corruption, bribery, theft and tax evasion cost developing countries approximately $1.26 trillion [USD] per year.

Love Data or Not, I Have an Idea for You

Setting aside the above data for a moment, remember that these figures represent the kids with yellow paper crowns I met in Bihar, India. And they represent their fathers and mothers, who each day wake up wondering if they will have enough food for their children today or how long it will be until the water they're drinking will kill them. They wonder if their kids can stay enrolled in school or if they will have to pull them out to help the family earn a living to survive. They don't know how they will afford the medical care they need or if they will ever achieve their goals. These are *real* people.

When I talk about the impoverished closest to my heart, the people of Bihar, India, it's difficult for me—painful even. Because they're not numbers to me or photos. They are people who have placed their hands in mine and asked for prayer. I have seen the suffering in their eyes. I have heard their stories and wept with them. But I also get to be the one who watches Jesus renew their communities and their lives. I get to be the one who can have hope with them. I get to be the one to hear about the joy of overcoming great odds—and witness the incredible bravery required to do so. I get to see hope, hearts, and homes renewed.

As you read the rest of this book, I ask that you would diligently and prayerfully discern which people group is your Bihar, India. We are all together in this effort, and we will all share in the consequences if we fail to take action.

I know that God wants to mightily use *you* to empower people to overcome spiritual and physical poverty. And I know that He wants to use you to make the world a better place—starting locally among people impoverished in your city and extending globally among the extreme poor. Any step in the right direction is better than doing nothing. God can magnify our efforts, no matter how small. My prayer is that you will reject the apathy so common in our culture. Embrace Christ's love for the world. Join with Him in changing lives in this world and changing souls toward eternal life with Him.

WHY POVERTY CONTINUES

The reason extreme poverty continues to affect people, even after funds are poured into communities, is actually quite simple: there is a lack of a holistic plan—a focus on the *physical only* by some groups and the *spiritual only* by others. Sustainable solutions are frequently overlooked in favor of quick fixes. The spiritual issue of corruption prevents good work from making a long-term difference.

Compounding the problem is that organizations and churches often refuse to work together for fear of losing control, influence, or donor bases. This is not God's vision for how Christians should work together. God desires collaboration. (See, for example, 1 Corinthians 12:12–31.) We must work *together* to create change in communities across the globe. And our work must be *holistic*.

The nonprofit Jesus' Economy aims to tackle the issues of poverty alleviation by *combining* job creation, church planting, and meeting basic needs. The idea is to renew a community by meeting spiritual and physical needs in a sustainable way. This is the *holistic* model.

A Chance to Escape Poverty—Creating Jobs

There's no doubt that job creation is the number one solution for sustainable poverty alleviation. When a person has a job, they can create a plan for their lives—a plan that doesn't rely on regular financial assistance from other people to sustain it. Jobs give dignity and independence.

That is why the Bible emphasizes the importance of work to our well-being. (See, for example, 1 Thessalonians 4:11; 2 Thessalonians 3:10–12.)

But how can we create sustainable jobs? How can we create cycles of economic development that *actually* lift people out of poverty?

In the developing world, sustainable job creation seems nearly impossible. Often, local political corruption, combined with the overall problems affiliated with living in extreme poverty conditions, deteriorates whatever progress is being made. This is why microloans, with the global marketplace in mind, are key to economic development.

Microloans can be offered in a variety of contexts, but they are generally offered to people living below the poverty line, who have little or no collateral. Microloans are an alternative to traditional bank or business loans, intended to fill the gap for people who could not obtain financing otherwise. For example, the organization Jesus' Economy raises funds for impoverished women in rural India who intend to multiply their businesses. After an initial business training, they will be eligible to receive a loan of $500 to $1,000 to purchase supplies for expanding their businesses. Microloans also vary from traditional loans in that they may not have traditional repayment schedules and can be interest-free. Some organizations, such as Jesus' Economy, reinvest the funds in future microloans when a loan is repaid.

But microloans alone are not enough. For economies to truly transform, we need to see job markets, basic necessities, and ethical health as interrelated. We need to see the physical person and the spiritual person as one and the same.

If you can provide someone with a microloan and business training, and then ensure that fair trade and ethical standards are met—while connecting that same person to a global marketplace—economies will quickly transform. I call this *microloans with e-commerce in mind* or *microloans with our interconnected globe in mind*. This is a pivotal aspect of creating jobs, particularly in a developing-world context. In this model, money from a *developed* economy can enter a *developing* economy in a sustainable way.

The wealth gap is a major problem in our world; it is a contributing factor to the wars and violence we witness every year. But how do we change it? One way is to create investment in developing economies. We create a reason for people from the *developed* world to buy from or invest in businesses in the *developing* world. We create market opportunities and market interest. (Presidents Clinton and Obama both launched initiatives like this for US trade and investment in African economies.)

These investments should benefit the long-term health of the community. (Contrast this with the often-devastating effects of resource mining or corporate investments that benefit only the ruling class.) After the market is established, it must be maintained: that's where training, continual access to larger markets, and accountability come together.

An Opportunity to Alleviate Corruption— Creating Churches

Jobs are only sustainable when corruption is eradicated from a community—and the clearest way to end corruption is to affirm the role of Jesus in people's lives.

Although Christians can be as susceptible to sin as anyone else, when we truly allow the Holy Spirit to lead our lives, corruption has no place. The church should be an instrument for good in this world—a spiritual health barometer, detecting injustice and instability. Positive change in a community can (and should) find its origins in the body of Christ.

Jesus did not tell His disciples to leave the world, but to be part of it— and to be vehicles of change *in it*. Jesus made this point in His final prayer for His disciples:

> I do not ask that you take them [the disciples] out of the world, but that you protect them from the evil one. They are not of the world, just as I am not of the world. Sanctify them in the truth—your word is truth. Just as you sent me into the world, I also have sent them into the world.   (John 17:15–18)

Jesus' disciples soon took this message and applied it to the newly created church. It is the church that should most acutely show God's truth in the world—that He truly loves people and that He wants all people to fully overcome spiritual and physical poverty. The church must be the epicenter of poverty alleviation.

All over the world, there are incredible church planters just waiting for funding. At Jesus' Economy, we get dozens of emails per week asking for support. We don't have the finances to fund most of them, but we wish we did.

Financial struggle is the story of nearly every missionary effort from every time period—even today. We have to ask ourselves, "Why is that? Is it possible that we are placing financial value on the wrong things?"

There are over 950 people groups in the world *without* missionaries (according to Finishing the Task).[3] It is estimated that 99.7 percent of the church's resources—its missional activities and financial support—are dedicated to areas where the church is *already* present; that means only 0.3 percent of resources are dedicated to where the church is *not* present (according to Issachar Initiative).[4] Over 41 percent of the world's population—that's over three billion people—have not heard Jesus' name or have little to no access to the gospel (according to The Joshua Project).[5] Let that number sink in.

Sometimes, where there are churches, those churches are sick with corruption, uneducated leadership, or lack of funding. A healthy church can serve as a hub for compassionate ministry. Often, all that is needed for a church to become healthy is additional biblical training and mentorship.

A healthy church is a chance to spiritually change a community. It is a chance to fight corruption with the love and ethics of Jesus.

---

3. "Finishing the Task Progress," Finishing the Task, https://www.finishingthetask.com/stats.htm (accessed September 19, 2018).

4. "Issachar Initiative, Extending the Reach of the Church," Issachar Initiative, https://issacharinitiative.org/about/ (accessed April 4, 2018); "Which Ministry Activities and Resources Extend the Kingdom?" Issachar Initiative, https://issacharinitiative.org/about/ (accessed April 4, 2018).

5. "Global Statistics," The Joshua Project, https://joshuaproject.net/people_groups/statistics (accessed September 19, 2018).

A Means to End Solvable Suffering— Meeting Basic Needs

Many physical poverty issues *are solvable*. If we combine job and church creation—while solving the problem of daily suffering because of a lack of basic needs—*we could see entire societies renewed*.

Think of how beautiful it would be if *indigenous leaders* created jobs and churches for their own communities, while meeting basic needs. What if those of us in the world with more wealth provided the funding, and other resources, necessary to launch these initiatives?

It is my hope that organizations everywhere would embrace a *holistic model* of alleviating poverty. And that those of us around the world would see the value in overcoming spiritual and physical poverty in each of our communities—in a sustainable way—and empowering other communities to do the same.

This all starts with *you* and with *me*. I hope you decide to *really* love someone today by walking with people on their way out of poverty and working with them toward sustainability. Help instill biblical ethics into your community to ensure stability and empower others to do the same. In the process, I am betting that you will find, as I have, that it helps alleviate some of your own spiritual poverty.

We have an opportunity to bring hope to people in desperate situations. Now is the time to show *true* compassion.

WE'RE ALL CONNECTED

"Love your neighbor as yourself" (Matthew 19:19). Following this teaching seems simple at first, but think about it for a moment. How do I *really love* someone as myself? Jesus is asking us to be *truly compassionate*. He wants us to realize how *interconnected* we all are.

What we do and how we act affects everyone around us—both locally and abroad. We are not only emotionally and spiritually connected but also economically linked to our brothers and sisters around the world, thanks to the technological advances of the twenty-first century.

What we do with our wealth here affects what happens across the globe and vice versa. Just ask a stock trader or a gas station owner, and you will find out that prices fluctuate in your local area based on events or sales that took place thousands of miles away.

Due to an increase in immigration to Western countries and the relocation of refugees after massive conflicts in Asia and Africa, our communities are becoming more diverse than they have ever been. We are seeing a blend of faces and cultures rarely seen together in previous generations. The technological revolution has contributed to this reality by creating digital connections between our existing trade connections. The Internet age has brought us all into the reality of a globally inter-connected life.

The easiest cultural example of this phenomenon is the rise of Facebook and subsequent social media platforms. Now we can literally converse face-to-face with someone across the globe as if we were standing in the same room. Never before in all of history has this been possible. Our world is truly interconnected.

Interconnection Means New Opportunities

An interconnected world, with interconnected people, opens up new possibilities for positive change.

Think of how rapidly we can fund projects, tell stories of incredible heroes of Christianity, report on news, or create businesses to fund transformation. We can connect Christians everywhere—and in doing so, connect and unify the church for the purpose of overcoming spiritual and physical poverty.

This type of positive change will have a compounding effect. When Christ changes the life of one person, it opens up the possibility for that person to change the lives of others. The effect continues, rippling outward. When we empower one person, we make it so that they can empower others. Nearly every Christian today has experienced this compounding effect. Jesus ministered to His disciples two thousand years ago, and today, Christianity is global. Only God knows exactly how this has happened over time, but from one person to the next, the message was brought to us. You never know the effect that one conversation, or one investment in someone else, will have.

When we forget our connection to others and the purpose of our relationships, we lose sight of the purpose of our lives: to bless the world in Jesus' name. (See Genesis 12:1–3; Matthew 28:18–20.)

If We Really Want to Solve This Problem...

Despite the fact that our world is more connected now than it has ever been, poverty rates are still astounding. It's tempting to ask questions like "How could this be?" or "Why do people have to suffer?" but we know the answers—it all comes down to what we do and don't do for others.

It's easy to be angry about the suffering of humanity and point fingers at God or others, until we realize that the problems of humanity are truly rooted in all of us. This has been the case since the day that Adam and Eve chose to turn against God. (See Genesis 3.)

Solving our problems—the absence of basic sanitation, dirty water, hindrances to addressing curable and preventable diseases, corrupt governments, poor infrastructure, and a lack of job creation, to name a few—means first looking to God for wisdom and then realizing that God is looking directly back at us to act.

God empowers us to do the work. As broken as humans are, we are still Jesus' hands and feet in the world. (See, for example, 1 Corinthians 12:12–31.) We have to take ownership of our responsibility to help those less fortunate than ourselves, to truly love our neighbor.

Lest we think that it's not possible for us to do this, we must remember first that nothing is impossible with God (see, for example, Matthew 17:19–20), and second how much we have already overcome. A drastic dent has been made in the extreme poverty problem already. There is more awareness of the issues people are facing around the globe than there has ever been. And more money is being put toward poverty-related problems than we have ever seen. But more is left to do.

No Limit to Our Potential

In this interconnected age, there is no limit to the potential of humanity for good (or evil). We have a unique opportunity to leverage awareness, websites, and something as simple as how we shop, to transform lives. We can leverage what's happening in our world for good.

Together, we have an opportunity to make people who feel completely isolated—struggling and alone—not just feel connected but actually *be* connected to the global community. In the process, we can implement new levels of transparency and accountability.

It may seem like a crazy dream to speak of hope for our entire world. But I believe we can employ the technology and interconnected economy of our world to make that hope real.

Reflections on Part One:
Jesus Is the Key to Overcoming Poverty

When God calls us to something great, we are immediately confronted by a faith decision: how will we respond? Accordingly, when we go about alleviating poverty, we're placing faith in *what can be*. We're imagining a better future for our world. As Jesus calls us to help the impoverished, He expects a faith-based and faithful response.

From the beginning of our faith walk until its end in this life, our journey is about *being in* this world as actors of change. Faith is not a journey that is about *removing* ourselves from this place, but one about bringing God's kingdom *to* this place. It's praying, "May your kingdom come,…as it is in heaven" (Matthew 6:10).

God has given us a chance to empower people, so that together we can change the course of history for the better. This is the *faithful* response.

What we do with faith is as important as our coming to faith, for what we do once we come to Jesus is what makes a difference in the lives of others. It's where change for the betterment of our world occurs. And what change does God envision? I think it is one in which we care deeply about spiritual and physical poverty, seeing it all as connected. God envisions a future where we, as a collective humanity, invite Him to renew our communities.

Put simply, Jesus is the real key to overcoming poverty. He is the reason why we live and why we love.

Let's learn from Jesus and the Scriptures He read, and from His earliest followers. Let's look to the rest of Scripture to see what hope, dreams, peace, and faith look like when it comes to poverty.

PART TWO

God's view of the impoverished.
What the Bible says about poverty.
And what that *really* means.

JESUS WILL SHOCK YOU

"I was a construction manager making good money; then my wife and kids died in a car accident. I couldn't hold it together. I couldn't move on after they were gone. I couldn't work. I couldn't sleep. I could barely eat. Before I knew it, my bank account was empty and that's how I ended up here." Standing inside a homeless shelter, staring into the tearful eyes of an older man I had stereotyped as a pothead who hadn't stopped smoking since the 1970s, I realized, "There is only one step between him and me." He didn't drink, smoke, or do drugs—he never had. We were the same.

I wanted to help, but his needs went beyond my capacity, and a small handout wouldn't change anything. Those of us with cash often don't realize that our financial charity can actually be toxic, as author and nonprofit leader Robert Lupton and others have taught us. (In addition, if previous ministry experience hadn't taught me to just listen, my counsel could have hurt my new friend at the homeless shelter.)

Around the world, people are now looking for better, empowering methods for alleviating poverty. To carry on Lupton's ideas, let's answer the question, "How would Jesus help?" I think Jesus' answers may shock you and bring tears to your own eyes.

We've Yet to Learn What Giving Really Looks Like

It's much easier to hand a homeless person a food card or some money than it is to sit down with them, hear their story, and help them find shelter or a job.

When we give quickly, without thought, we are often ignoring the key relational aspects of ministry. Sometimes our motives are less than pure. Do we not often hope that people, and their problems, will just go away? Do people in need make us uncomfortable about our current or desired life choices? I don't know about you, but I've certainly felt such emotions. Where do those emotions come from? Is there a better way to approach giving?

If we believe the "neighbor" Jesus calls us to love (see, for example, Luke 10:27) is any and every person, then we should also believe that people deserve our time and attention. Although sometimes all a person really needs is a few dollars, our mode of operation should be relational, not transactional. Everyone deserves the opportunity to tell their story and be loved *as an entire person*, not just *a need*.

Jesus is seemingly spontaneous in His acts of service (all the random miracles), but He is also serious about His relationships. We see Jesus repeatedly eating with people and stopping for discussions and questions. Here is God in the flesh, with the limitation of having only three years of ministry time on earth, stopping to eat, drink, and have conversation. (See, for example, Luke 18:35–43.) This is how He works.

Jesus also stops to get to know those who are considered unlovable by His culture, like the Samaritan woman at the well. (See John 4:1–26.) And in doing so, He keeps the focus on what God plans to do in their lives—He instills not just help but hope. He empowers them to receive true freedom in Him.

Serve Always—and That Means Listening

Most of us like to believe we're right most of the time. And we all like to have solutions for other people's problems, especially when it's not up to us to implement them. We're quick to assume we know what our hurting friends need and to tell them so, but James says, "Every person must be quick to hear, slow to speak" (James 1:19).

Many of us—I say "us," because I used to do this too—assume that the homeless who are not mentally, developmentally, or physically disabled, are simply lazy. This can't be farther from the truth. Our misplaced beliefs about the hurting can even make us angry.

Jesus has some strong words about viewing others in such ways: "But I say to you that everyone who is angry at his brother will be subject to judgment, and whoever says to his brother, 'Stupid fool!' will be subject to the council, and whoever says, 'Obstinate fool!' will be subject to fiery hell" (Matthew 5:22). That's Jesus—He continues to shock me.

"The Poor You Always Have with You," so Don't Forget Jesus

Christianity is about self-sacrifice, but if it isn't for Jesus' glory and purposes, there really isn't a point to it. We have all heard the saying, "It's all about Jesus." We would love to tell others we believe it. Yet, our actions often say we don't.

For Jesus, the most important outcome possible is the glory of God. When on earth, He profoundly understood that everything, and I mean everything, should be connected back to that. He also understood that the connection to God's glory would come through His work on the cross, as the Savior of God's people. When we realize this, Jesus' reasoning for allowing a woman to spend an entire expensive perfume flask on Him makes sense. Those around Jesus scolded the woman, because the perfume could have been sold to help the poor. Jesus rebuked them, saying, "For the poor you always have with you, and you can do good for them whenever you want, but you do not always have me" (Mark 14:7). Jesus is foremost.

That is not to say that we should focus only on spreading the gospel and forsake people's needs. After all, think of what the letter of James says:

> If a brother or sister is poorly clothed and lacking in daily food, and one of you says to them, "Go in peace, be warmed and filled," without giving them the things needed for the body, what good is that? So also faith by itself, if it does not have works, is dead.
> (James 2:15–17 esv)

If we contextualize Jesus in the way His disciple James did, we see what Jesus means by "the poor you always have with you." Jesus is telling us to alleviate poverty *within* relationship. And that relationship should *emerge out of* our love for Jesus. Our relationship with Jesus is *primary*, and that primary relationship prompts us to *truly love* other people.

Life change can happen in a wide variety of contexts, through Christian and non-Christian organizations alike. But life change that also involves the good news of Jesus is eternal. Jesus is calling us to contextualize temporal needs within our eternal relationship with God.

But Remember, "In the Poor, You Find Me"

Entering into relationship is challenging, especially when power dynamics like income level are involved. You may find people living in poverty to be unrelatable. You might find yourself feeling uncomfortable when speaking with them. I do not assume here that we are all coming from a position of wealth. On the other side of the coin, you may find those with wealth to be pretentious or putting themselves on a pedestal. You may find yourself judging their intentions.

Most of us have experienced both of these types of emotions. What's important is that we stop and name that feeling in ourselves and ask: "How can I use power well, in a way that honors others?" "How can I deal with people using power over me, in a way that honors how God wants me to live?"

The answer to those questions is complicated, but we must remember that all people were created in the image of God. (See Genesis 1:26–27.) We are all equals in His sight. (See Galatians 3:28–29.) God does not distinguish between rich and poor. "Rich and poor have much in common; Yahweh is the maker of all of them" (Proverbs 22:2).

The question is, "What are we going to do with what we have been given?" No matter our position of power and wealth, or lack thereof, how will we treat people who are marginalized or outside of our community?

In the midst of discussing forthcoming judgment, Jesus uses our view of "the other" as a distinguishing factor between those who truly believe and those who don't. He goes so far as to say that when we help the hungry, the thirsty, the stranger, the naked, the sick, and the imprisoned, we are actually doing those things *for* Him. (See Matthew 25:31–46.)

Jesus cares about how you give, why you give, and how you treat people. If we care about what Jesus cares about, we must listen to what He has to say about our duty to serve others. It turns out that Jesus gives us a lot of tips that will help us avoid some of the pitfalls that can turn our good intentions into horrible mistakes.

WHAT JESUS *REALLY* SAID ABOUT POVERTY

In Jesus, God came as a poor man, lived as a poor man, and died as a poor man. He is good news to the poor. And as such, Jesus cares deeply about the impoverished.

Jesus is all about loving others with everything you have, in every moment, in proclamation of the eternal life He offers. Here are some statements in which Jesus directly speaks about the impoverished (all from the ESV translation). As you read them, reflect upon what He is saying to *you*—about your spiritual and physical poverty.

> For you always have the poor with you, but you will not always have me. (Matthew 26:11)

> You lack one thing: go, sell all that you have and give to the poor, and you will have treasure in heaven; and come, follow me. (Mark 10:21)

> Truly, I say to you, this poor widow has put in more than all those who are contributing to the offering box. (Mark 12:43)

> The Spirit of the Lord is upon me, because he has anointed me to proclaim good news to the poor. He has sent me to proclaim liberty to the captives and recovering of sight to the blind, to set at liberty those who are oppressed. (Luke 4:18)

Blessed are you who are poor, for yours is the kingdom of God.
(Luke 6:20)

Go and tell John what you have seen and heard: the blind receive their sight, the lame walk, lepers are cleansed, and the deaf hear, the dead are raised up, the poor have good news preached to them.
(Luke 7:22)

But when you give a feast, invite the poor, the crippled, the lame, the blind.
(Luke 14:13)

The more I read Jesus' sayings about the impoverished, and the contexts surrounding them, the more He changes my worldview. I am constantly learning from Jesus what it means to fully love others and give of myself. I try to pray each day that He will teach me to better live His sayings. Let's reflect together on a few of these sayings and see where that leads us. He speaks to our beliefs and the empathy that should accompany them.

Being What We Believe

Jesus is about complete commitment to loving Him and others. He loves belief-filled actions, as His saying to a wealthy young man shows: "If you want to be perfect, go, sell your possessions and give the proceeds to the poor—and you will have treasure in heaven—and come, follow me" (Matthew 19:21). The man walks away sorrowful. (See verse 22.) Jesus then makes one of His most famous statements:

Truly I say to you that with difficulty a rich person will enter into the kingdom of heaven! And again I say to you, it is easier for a camel to go through the eye of a needle than a rich person into the kingdom of God.
(Matthew 19:23–24)

Jesus' disciples ask, "Then who can be saved?" (verse 25). Jesus looks at them and says, "With human beings this is impossible, but with God all things are possible" (verse 26). Jesus is not suggesting it is impossible for a rich person to enter the kingdom of heaven, or be saved—He is saying it is *only* possible with God. And for God to enter a person's life, they must be open to Him entering.

Many of us are just like the rich young man. Out of one side of our mouth, we speak allegiance to Jesus, but out of the other side, we're speaking allegiance to the trappings of wealth. I know, because the rich young man asks the same questions I would ask. Look at the events that prompted Jesus to make His statement about the wealthy:

> And behold, someone [the rich young man] came up to him and said, "Teacher, what good thing must I do so that I will have eternal life?" And he said to him, "Why are you asking me about what is good? There is one who is good. But if you want to enter into life, keep the commandments!" He said to him, "Which ones?" And Jesus said, "Do not commit murder, do not commit adultery, do not steal, do not give false testimony, honor your father and your mother, and love your neighbor as yourself." The young man said to him, "All these I have observed. What do I still lack?"
>
> (Matthew 19:16–20)

Jesus is clearly frustrated and perhaps even offended: "Why are you asking me about what is good?" The man is asking the wrong question. He doesn't ask how he can follow Jesus, or what it means to be a disciple—or what good thing he can do for the world on behalf of a good God. He asks, "What good thing must I do so that I will have eternal life?" If we're honest with ourselves, isn't that the question many of us are asking God today? Jesus is unsatisfied with that question.

Eternal life (salvation) is God's great gift, but it's meant to be a gift that prompts action. It is meant to give us purpose. It is meant to free us, so that we may have a deep and fruitful relationship with God—be a true disciple of Jesus—and take action on His behalf by loving other people.

When I was confronted with the reality of the story of the rich young man, I asked another question that the young man asked after Jesus told him, "Keep the commandments!": "Which ones?" Jesus cites to the man all the relational Ten Commandments, and in doing so, basically implies, "All of them." The man tells Jesus he has observed these and then asks,

"What do I still lack?" It is this question that gets to the root of the issue. Jesus tells the man that he lacks self-sacrifice for others—he lacks giving to the extent that it is painful to him. He lacks an ability to put aside his wealth for the sake of the gospel. Wealth is meant to bless others—plain and simple. (See, for example, Genesis 12:1–3.) It is not for hoarding, and it will—if not given up, when God prompts you—keep you from fully experiencing the blessings of God.

But do not fear or worry—instead, pray. Remember, "with human beings this is impossible, but with God all things are possible." Jesus said that in the context of this very scene, because He knows how difficult it is for us. It is painful to embrace Jesus over and against all the other things we put ahead of Him. He knows that without God's power, it is impossible to *truly* change our lives.

Giving Even When You Don't Have Much

It is not just the wealthy who are called by Jesus to give. Giving is something we all must practice. It is one of the ways we overcome the spiritual poverty of our hearts and alleviate the physical poverty of others in the process. And this idea is even more profound when practiced by the impoverished.

Regarding an impoverished widow who put a seemingly insignificant amount of money into the offering box (see Mark 12:41–44), Jesus says:

> Truly, I say to you, this poor widow has put in more than all those who are contributing to the offering box. For they all contributed out of their abundance, but she out of her poverty has put in every- thing she had, all she had to live on.   (verses 43–44 ESV)

Jesus' Currency

The currency of Jesus' kingdom is different from ours. Jesus' economy is based on self-sacrifice and His currency is love. For Jesus, belief and actions are one and the same—you cannot have one without the other.

The more I reflect on the problem of poverty and what Jesus has to say about it, the more I realize that we own the problems of the impoverished as much as they do. Our inactions have created many of those problems. We—all of us—are at fault for the state of our world. But we can also join Jesus in changing the state of our world.

If Jesus believes that faith is about action, then why don't we? Why have we not dedicated ourselves to bringing true discipleship and love to others, when it's what Christ tells us to do? What good is belief if it does not offer true hope?

Hope Is About Believing What Is Yet to Be

For Jesus—like the author of Hebrews (see Hebrews 11:1)—hope is about believing in what is yet to be and acting on that belief. We are called to follow Jesus with our entire being. The results of doing so are incredible.

Right at the beginning of the gospel of Mark, we see the power of Jesus' calling upon our lives:

> Passing alongside the Sea of Galilee, [Jesus] saw Simon and Andrew the brother of Simon casting a net into the sea, for they were fishermen. And Jesus said to them, "Follow me, and I will make you become fishers of men." And immediately they left their nets and followed him. And going on a little farther, he saw James the son of Zebedee and John his brother, who were in their boat mending the nets. And immediately he called them, and they left their father Zebedee in the boat with the hired servants and followed him. (Mark 1:16–20 ESV)

Jesus' earliest followers literally dropped their livelihoods to follow Him—they completely dedicated themselves to Him. Similarly, we are called to make sacrifices for Jesus—to show others love by giving, praying, and investing in them.

To a man who recently lost a loved one, Jesus says, "Follow me!" (Luke 9:59). But the man replies:

> "Lord, let me first go and bury my father." And Jesus said to him, "Leave the dead to bury their own dead. But as for you, go and proclaim the kingdom of God." (verses 59–60 ESV)

For Jesus, it's all about God's kingdom. For us, also, it should be all about God's kingdom. From a different man, Jesus hears this response:

"I will follow you, Lord, but let me first say farewell to those at my home." Jesus said to him, "No one who puts his hand to the plow and looks back is fit for the kingdom of God."

(Luke 9:61–62 ESV)

There should be no hesitations in service to God's kingdom and no looking back—it's all about what God is doing here and now. It's all about putting our hand to the plow of God's work. If you love God, you love the kingdom and you love people. If you love the kingdom, you're not going to ask yourself what else might be more important: you're going to just live for the kingdom, as Jesus' earliest disciples did. Peter echoes this sentiment following the incident with the rich young man, saying, "Behold, we have left everything and followed you. What then will there be for us?" (Matthew 19:27). There must have been no guile in Peter's question, for Jesus responds incredibly positively:

Truly I say to you that in the renewal of the world, when the Son of Man sits on his glorious throne, you who have followed me—you also will sit on twelve thrones judging the twelve tribes of Israel. And everyone who has left houses or brothers or sisters or father or mother or wife or children or fields on account of my name will receive a hundred times as much, and will inherit eternal life. But many who are first will be last, and the last first. (Matthew 19:28–30)

Put simply, applying Jesus' teachings today means withdrawing from any relationship, occupation, event, or thing that stands between us and following Jesus. When we do so, we must also honor the other commandments Jesus tells the rich young man: "Do not commit murder, do not commit adultery, do not steal, do not give false testimony, honor your father and your mother, and love your neighbor as yourself" (Matthew 19:18–19).

Jesus has called us to join Him in His work—to believe in it with *all we have*. The cost may be hard to bear or even understand at times, but when it is put in the perspective of all that Christ has done for us—dying for our sins—and all that we will receive in His kingdom, it seems like very little.

God has asked us to demonstrate our belief by bringing good news to those who feel hopeless. This is what the concept of Jesus' economy is all about: envisioning what the world could look like and joining God in the process of making that vision a reality. It's about exchanging the various currencies of this world—wealth, power, and comfort—for the currency of love. And when we make this decision, it allows for us to have empathy like never before.

Jesus and Empathy

For those of us who have much, it is difficult to understand the lives of those who have little. We have trouble fully comprehending what life is like on the other side of the poverty line. But we're closer to understanding than we might think.

Jesus is the person who brings us closer; He is the source of our empathy. My clue for this comes from passages like this:

> As they were going along the road, someone said to [Jesus], "I will follow you wherever you go." And Jesus said to him, "Foxes have holes, and birds of the air have nests, but the Son of Man has nowhere to lay his head." (Luke 9:57–58 ESV)

Jesus lived like the impoverished we wish to empower: He had "nowhere to lay his head." There is sadness in this statement, but there is also hope. It makes me sad for Jesus, but in my empathy for Christ, I am learning to have increasing empathy for those who are hurting. I am growing closer to God's heart as I think upon Jesus' plight.

And this is much of what believing in Jesus is all about: we have an opportunity to recognize how God Himself experienced the full spectrum of suffering through His Son, Jesus, and then do as Christ did—give of ourselves freely for the betterment of others.

There is hope for those living in poverty. There is love to be offered. There is empathy to be found for each and every situation. There is empathy to be felt and experienced through our relationship with Jesus.

It is in Christ, who experienced poverty, that we also find the solution to poverty. We find new life through His resurrection. We find hope in Him that we can offer to others. We find order overtaking chaos. We find death itself not being able to hold back God's work. We see an overcoming of all things that tear at the fabric of what humanity was originally meant to be. We see a restoration of life. We see lives lived fully for the eternal God, starting now. There is power to be found in this kind of empathy. But having true empathy isn't easy.

JESUS NEVER SAID IT WOULD BE EASY

"He's dead." The words stung like the icy water in which I had baptized my now dead friend, less than a year before. "What happened?" I thought. It was all so shocking, overwhelming, and painful. "How did we fail him?"

Kevin had been on track. He'd had a job and been enrolled in community college. He had overcome addiction and past pain and victimization, and had gone through an incredible program via a rescue mission to do so. We weren't worried about him—but we should have been.

We later learned that, essentially, a welfare check and government-provided free rent had killed Kevin. He had discovered that to get a larger welfare check and government housing, he would have to stop working to bring his income bracket down. Astonishingly, Kevin would have more spending money that way. So, he quit his job and shortly thereafter quit community college. Then, Kevin was hit with the news that his mother had died. With no stability system left—thanks to Kevin's newfound independence, he had cut ties to his accountability relationship with the rescue mission staff—he went back to drugs, for one night only. Kevin sought the same level of high as previously, and that was enough to kill him. (His body was no longer acclimated to the drugs, and the shock of the high crashed his system.)

Would Jesus Discuss This?

When I start talking about the problems people like Kevin experience—how I feel the U.S. welfare system fails them in many areas—people get uncomfortable. This can all seem like something we would rather not discuss. But the brokenness of a government-run system that exists apart from Christ's influence is self-evident.

Please know that I am not advocating against the separation of church and state. History has shown us that the marriage of religion and government lends itself to all kinds of temptation and, ultimately, corruption. I am merely saying that Christians should be the number one specialists for loving the *whole person*, as Christ has taught us to do.

That means that we should be absolute experts at helping people overcome sins that are causing them to repeat destructive cycles in their lives and in the lives of their children. This is often called "generational poverty," or "self-inflicted poverty cycles" that are repeated generation after generation.

The government is not in the business of telling people that their sin is costing them their lives. And it doesn't usually welcome people into community or provide accountability relationships.

I have heard stories of people like Kevin who try to change their lives. They get a job and search for housing, but as soon as they make too much money, the government calls to collect. It is cheaper for them to not have a job, and to let the government pay for their food and shelter.

I have been to low-income housing units that were designated specifically for the homeless—a great idea in principle—but no one enforced an alcohol- or drug-free environment (or common courtesy). The apartments were trashed. People had urinated and written on the walls. They had no respect for the property because they did nothing to earn it.

I've also been in government-sponsored halfway shelters, heard people's stories of loss and devastation, and been told that I cannot share the gospel with them. In these situations, I ask myself, "Are a meal card and some free baby products really going to change these people's lives? Are these things really going to save them from the cycles of addiction they are in or the severe depression they are facing?"

I am not saying that I am against government social programs, such as housing, food stamps, or even welfare. My point is that the American system is clearly broken and the underlying reason is spiritual.

People like Kevin will continue to die at the hands of badly constructed systems if we don't act on their behalf. No doubt, my friend had a choice, but the money in his bank account—supplied by the welfare system—made his bad decisions too easy.

If loving a whole person rather than just handing them a check was what we all did, Kevin likely would not have died. If well-intentioned Christians—who no doubt had a hand in crafting the welfare system—had made the decision that handouts weren't good enough (and were demeaning), Kevin might still be alive. I don't think Jesus would have tolerated the pejorative treatment of the impoverished that is common to our welfare system.

Aside from how controversial it feels, Jesus—and what He would have us to do—should be the subject of our lives, even if that means accepting difficult truths and making hard decisions.

There Are No Easy Answers

Jesus being our focus means admitting that there are no easy answers. And it means confessing when we have failed people—including directly stating what we have done that has hurt them. It means walking away from the easy choice (throwing money at the problem) and deciding to take on the difficult task of holistically loving someone.

Jesus being the center means our standing against systems that destroy lives and providing a substitute that's focused on loving the entire person and entire communities.

TRULY UNDERSTANDING THE ALWAYS-PERPLEXING JESUS

He was impassioned and noticeably angry. Then he said boldly, "They're killing my people." This director of a rescue mission to the homeless was fed up with the careless treatment of the homeless in his community. His declaration came on the heels of this remark: "Somebody bought him his last drink by giving him some money when he begged for it on the street." The man had died from alcohol poisoning later that night.

From nearly anyone working directly with the homeless population in the U.S., you will hear that government programs and handouts don't work. Meet one of these people on the front line of this very difficult work and you will be told that many of the things we believe are right in principle—like giving someone money when they ask—don't work in practice.

This is difficult to digest when you've heard your whole life that you should give freely, without thought—this was the message I heard growing up in megachurches. How could I connect Jesus with what I was learning?

As you probably know, Jesus is a total radical when it comes to helping other people. Jesus' ideas about charity and giving are directly connected to His ideas about loving others. For Jesus, giving does not concern just your checkbook; it's a lifestyle. Of course, this is most apparent in Jesus' sacrificial style of living—He died on a cross for other people—but His statements about giving are equally pressing.

Jesus the Generous, but Also the Just

Jesus directly states how He perceives charity:

> You have heard that it was said, "An eye for an eye and a tooth for a tooth." But I say to you, do not resist the evildoer, but whoever strikes you on the right cheek, turn the other to him also. And the one who wants to go to court with you and take your tunic, let him have your outer garment also. And whoever forces you to go one mile, go with him two. Give to the one who asks you, and do not turn away from the one who wants to borrow from you.   (Matthew 5:38–42)

At first glance, Jesus' words have a very direct application—give freely to others, and when someone wants to borrow from you, let them—but there are cultural issues at stake here, as well as larger principles to consider.

Jesus' culture was full of ramifications for wrongdoings that usually involved an exact exchange: you do this wrong thing to me and I will do the exact wrong thing back to you. This explains why Jesus uses the "eye for an eye" statement from Deuteronomy 19:21. He is setting us up to think within a particular framework. Then, Jesus exchanges this mind-set with an entirely different agenda. This rhetorical tactic is often called "the bait and switch." Comedy itself is based on this technique—setting an expectation and then breaking it. The surprise is what's funny.

The context indicates that Jesus is likely not making an ad-hoc, apply-to-all situations statement. Instead, He is directly addressing resentment and the assumption that you can issue justice on your own accord.

Jewish people in the first century AD issued punishment either by mob rulings or appealing to a local governing official. The two most obvious examples from Jesus' own lifetime are when some leaders attempt to punish a woman caught in adultery (see John 8:3–11) and when a mob attempts to push Jesus off of a cliff for what they perceive as heresy (see Luke 4:16–30). In their minds, "an eye for an eye," and laws like it, justified their vigilante behavior. It's every man for himself, under one Law (which was the first five books of the Bible); it's the wild, wild West, and if you wrong someone else, you will be stoned in the street.

It's within this culture that Jesus makes His statements about giving and debt. To interpret His statements separate from this context would be to make the same mistake that Jesus is arguing against—taking one verse (Deuteronomy 19:21) to apply to all situations, aside from the rest of God's revelation.

The focus, then, of Jesus' comments about giving and debt is primarily aimed at people who have wronged you. We could easily extend it to other situations, but before doing so, let's consider His main point.

When Jesus tells us to "give to the one who asks you," does He mean that we should give without any further thought? If our charity work has become damaging, should it continue? If a drunk comes up asking for money, should you give it to him?

This is where it's critical that we set aside our modern context for a moment. Unlike today, Jesus' day was not full of illegitimate panhandlers. Abusing alcohol was not the norm because wine was the main drink of choice. In a highly religious culture, over-consumption was not culturally acceptable. Drugs were not a part of that culture either. For the impoverished, there wasn't a social support system and structure, like welfare, and there weren't all the problems associated with it. There also weren't large-scale lending systems. Credit cards hadn't been invented yet, and there were no mortgages in the modern sense. Bankruptcy wasn't even a term. The government didn't bail you out. For good or bad, Jesus' day didn't have our systems or our lifestyles.

The societal norms of Jesus' day should also be considered when interpreting His comments about the poor and debt. It was completely and utterly humiliating to be poor: you were viewed as the least of society and generally thought to be a sinner. Not only was abusing a system or people's charity not an option, but being poor meant being the "loser" of the world. It was degrading and sad. The poor were left in poverty because they had no other options (unlike many of the U.S. poor). If I had been a poor man in Jesus' day, I likely wouldn't have become poor because I had made bad choices; rather, it would have been because I had a physical ailment or an incredibly bad lot, or I had been exploited by someone else. If my wife had been a poor woman in Jesus' lifetime, she likely would have been so because

I was already dead. As a widow, she would have had no other options but to beg. My family likely would not have had savings or investments for my widow to rely on because, in the first-century Roman Empire, most men only made enough to live on (if that).

Our world is a very different place. Systems of assistance have been established. There are charities that provide aid. Governments—for good or bad—support individuals who are economically at the bottom.

Jesus' statement "Give to the one who asks you"—like everything He says—should also be interpreted in light of His overall teaching to love God and others. (See, for example, Matthew 22:37–40.)

When Jesus tells us to "love our neighbor as ourselves," He is telling us to reconsider our primary daily thoughts about self-preservation, and, in the process, to think about things from another person's perspective. Can we really love our neighbor if our giving allows them to continue in self-destructive behavior or if it is damaging to the economy? Since it's not possible to love our neighbor and give to them without thought, then surely Jesus must have had a larger framework in mind when making His statements about giving.

We can give while also helping someone make good decisions. We can give while also helping to improve the physical and spiritual economy of a community. We can give freely without hurting others. We can help others without the danger of killing those we're trying to assist, while still honoring Jesus' commandments.

Some Things Never Change

Just as it's difficult to understand Jesus' view of giving, it's difficult to comprehend His view of debt. Both must be contextualized in terms of how we should love others, which is second only to loving God Himself.

Some things never change—praying about debt is one of them. In the same sermon where Jesus discusses giving and debt in light of justice, He brings up debt in light of prayer. When commenting on how to pray, Jesus says:

> But when you pray, do not babble repetitiously like the pagans, for they think that because of their many words they will be

heard. Therefore do not be like them, for your Father knows what you need before you ask him. Therefore you pray in this way: Our Father who is in heaven, may your name be treated as holy. May your kingdom come, may your will be done on earth as it is in heaven. Give us today our daily bread, and forgive us our debts, as we also have forgiven our debtors. And do not bring us into temptation, but deliver us from the evil one. For if you forgive people their sins, your heavenly Father will also forgive you. But if you do not forgive people, neither will your Father forgive your sins.   (Matthew 6:7–15)

As noted earlier, although part of this passage is often rendered "Forgive us our *trespasses*, as we forgive those who have *trespassed against us*," in the version of the Lord's Prayer in the gospel of Matthew, the original Greek literally uses the terms "debt" and "debtors."

From the subprime mortgage crisis, to bankruptcies, to overspending on home shopping networks using credit cards, we all know that debt can destroy lives. But it's not just this kind of debt Jesus is talking about. In His society, debt came in a form similar to the terms for loans offered by today's black market loan sharks.

Debts were usually created because of an unjust system and often involved victimization and exploitation. They almost always involved repayment schedules that could never be met and interest rates so astronomical that working for a lifetime was the only way to pay off the money owed. Metaphorically, and often literally, debt in the first-century AD enslaved people. Jesus desired freedom and dignity for those who had fallen into the trap of debt. He called His followers to forgive the debts owed to them, and thus create equality. He also instructed them to pray about the debts they owed to other people, essentially requesting God's intervention. And, Jesus acknowledged that everyone owed God debt for their sins—this is something He Himself repaid on our behalf by His death on a cross.

This contextualization makes me ask, "Would Jesus accept a system that gave someone dignity over one that does not?" Of course, Jesus would accept the system that offers dignity—and that's the true message of Jesus' view on debt.

Jesus' love and respect for people is unfathomable; He desires dignity for everyone. Often, when you give someone money outright, you eliminate their ability to feel empowered—in essence, you place them in the victim role. It's this mentality that Jesus is against.

But what would empowerment look like in practice? To use some modern alternatives to the "give freely without thought" mentality, let's briefly discuss microloans and grants.

APPLYING JESUS' ANCIENT TEACHINGS TO OUR MODERN CONTEXT

Jesus would have us correct societal ills—the sicknesses that help create poverty—such as corruption. But He would also have us do so out of authentic relationships. Jesus would have us consider how to rightly use our wealth in a way that honors those we're seeking to help. How then should we give?

Microloans and grants present us with intelligent giving options—they can, if used correctly, bring dignity back to the receiver of our gifts. They're a type of "give freely" option, but with more consideration built in.

Microloans, unlike standard loans, are not made to benefit the person lending the money. They're created to empower those receiving the loans, and the interest (if it is charged at all) is often reinvested in the system. When carried out properly, microloans are built on incredibly reasonable repayment schedules and rates. They are investments, and as such, are very different from ordinary debt. I believe they are the type of empowerment that Jesus would favor, and contextually, not the type of debt He opposed.

The Hope of a New Kind of Microloan

Microloans have proven to be a great source of hope in the developing world. And they may even be able to offer hope to the developed world. To date, microloans have been extremely effective. At one point, they were even believed to be the silver bullet for alleviating poverty. However, even a great idea can be improved upon. I believe we can offer even more hope by connecting microloans with e-commerce.

As I see it, there are five things that are holding back the effectiveness of microloans. Or, put in the positive, there are five points that we should consider about the future of microloans.

Five Points About the Future of Microloans

1. Microloans Alleviate Poverty Very Slowly

Economic reality dictates that microloans are a very slow way for someone to move out of poverty. Through a microloan, people may become self-sustaining quickly, but this does not mean they have moved out of poverty. Here's a way to understand the economics of a typical microloan in a developing-world community: If one poor tomato farmer sells their product to one poor butcher, the money is just exchanging hands and/or the profit margins are very slim for each. Their lives are significantly better, but not exponentially better. What developing communities really need is exponential economic growth.

Similarly, imagine that there is a poor seamstress, and we give her a loan to boost her business. Suddenly she has the money to buy better equipment and grow her business. She then goes to market and sells her products to a local laborer. But the laborer is relatively poor too. So what has happened? Money has simply exchanged hands. The laborer has given the poor seamstress some of his money. The seamstress is a little better off, but they're both still poor, and the economy has stayed the same.

Thus, if one poor person sells to another poor person, the economics of that community do *not* change. One person may rise out of poverty, or even a handful or a hundred, but the overall economic environment has not been transformed. Why? Because it is still a *local* economic effort, with money moving through the local economy. And wealth is not being created. But we can create wealth or at least move it from a wealthy economy to a poor economy, and there are greater opportunities to do so than ever before.

2. The World Is Online

A product-based business not connected to the Internet is missing a massive sector of the market. In developed economies, we wouldn't dream of launching a product-based business without an online presence. Most product-based companies in the U.S. sell online, yet we're somehow content with businesses in the developing world not doing the same. It is not logical to think that a business in the developing world will grow quickly without access to the rest of the world—global economics empower people. By connecting a developing-world business to online e-commerce, the business can grow faster; and that means more jobs.

3. Markets Dictate Quality

A product line is stronger when it is exposed to a larger market sector. Typically, the larger your market sector, the better your product needs to be, because there are more demands on your company from consumers. This puts the necessary pressure on a company to become stronger, faster, and more sustainable. This could happen for developing-world companies too, if they were connected to the Internet.

4. Microloans Have the Power to Create Jobs

While the typical microloan today has the power to create a *few* jobs in a community, it doesn't have the power to create a *lot* of jobs. To do that, you need more than just small companies; you need to create medium-to-large companies. Remember this fact from the United Nations Sustainable Development Goals:

> Small and medium-sized enterprises that engage in…manufacturing are the most critical for the early stages of industrialization and are typically the largest job creators. They make up over 90 percent of business worldwide and account for between 50–60 percent of employment.

So here's a solution: Imagine a developing-world company creating a product that many shoppers around the world desire. And then, imagine those shoppers being connected to the developing-world company via the Internet. Of course, to make this work, you need strong marketing and a network to fulfill orders in a place like the U.S.

But let's put aside all the logistics for a moment and just think about the possibility. What if a developing-world artisan had the guidance of U.S.-based entrepreneurs? What if developing-world entrepreneurs could be the ones to fulfill the various orders from U.S. businesses and U.S. customers? What if the Internet could connect business in this way?

That type of business could create not just a few jobs, but potentially hundreds, maybe thousands, of jobs. That type of business could leverage our global economy for the sake of the impoverished.

5. Bringing Products Together in One Marketplace Creates Buying Power

There's a basic reality of business that we all know to be true: a business needs customers. A large customer base is necessary for a company to grow rapidly, and it is rapid growth that developing-world businesses need. So here's an idea: what if we could find a way to market fair trade products better in the U.S.?

Now, at this point, you might hear someone say, "Well, certainly that is what Amazon and Walmart do." Not quite. Big, for-profit companies are, almost by necessity, all about pricing and, particularly, low prices. This can be good for the customer, but is it always good for the businesses they work with? (We don't need to go far to see that the ability to buy things cheaply costs someone, somewhere. This is the reality of the sweatshop.)

One may propose that the natural answer to this problem is the current global shopping networks. But Amazon and Walmart are not the answer for fair trade because their business models don't fit with what fair trade represents. What we need is an alternative marketplace (or marketplaces) for fair trade products.

Fair trade means that everyone is treated fairly: the customer and the product creator. What fair trade needs, then, is *a marketplace that is truly fair*—one that is not all about low price for the customer but instead about fair pricing for everyone.

Jesus' Economy, the organization, is working to create a large microloan program with e-commerce in mind. We're going to supplement this with the training of entrepreneurs, which will include biblical ethics instruction to help ensure that corruption does not destroy the investments we make. We plan to bring together entrepreneurs' products into one large marketplace—to create a network for fair trade online. All proceeds will be automatically reinvested in the work of Jesus' Economy. We believe that this will create lasting economic change in communities through sustainable job creation.

It is my hope that the entire nonprofit sector will get behind such ideas and that Christians everywhere will decide to buy fair trade for the purpose of job creation. It is my hope that we can collectively change our planet through enterprise. Microloans reimagined hold hope for our world. But, as discussed above, without the eradication of corruption, the effort won't matter. How, then, can we put an end to corruption? That's where direct grants, and specifically church grants, come in.

Grants: A Smarter Kind of Gift

Effective grants have built-in intelligence. They involve really knowing the needs of people and joining them in the process of creating positive change in the world.

Grants can be applied to a wide variety of contexts: from meeting basic needs, to funding church-planting efforts, to launching job-creation programs by establishing training centers. But the word *grant* implies a mutual relationship and accountability. And that's precisely what we need to alleviate poverty.

The most effective type of grant to alleviate poverty gets as close to the community in need as possible. This means the ideal grant recipient is a nonprofit or church working right in the community. This nonprofit or church should have community members driving the economic development process and the meeting of basic needs. This allows for a community to take ownership of the process. And who best knows what they need—an outsider or the locals? The answer is obviously the locals.

When it comes to grants, indigenous leadership is critical. Part of the reason why I believe so strongly in indigenous church planting is because a church planter can also function as a community developer. A church planter who speaks the local language and knows the local culture can stand in the center of economic development efforts and ensure that basic needs are appropriately met. But the church planter should not do this alone: they function like a facilitator of conversations and initiatives, which should be driven by the local community.

The reason why grants to local organizations are so effective is that they are built on relationships, involve clear project outlines, and hand over the development effort to people living where the work is taking place.

They can bypass corrupt government systems and, through accountability, ensure the effective use of funds.

There is a time to give, via a grant, and a time to make a loan, but both methods mean generosity. And both methods mean meeting someone where they're at, with dignity and intelligence. Grants require action, purpose, and reporting—they're not a handout. And microloans are investments that offer people the dignity of "owning" their own future.

A Place for Handouts?

Lest you misunderstand my argument against handouts, meaning spontaneous gifts of cash or goods to an un-vetted person or organization, please know that there are certainly moments when God will lead you to give spontaneously. The Spirit could very well tell you to hand all the cash in your wallet to someone who asks—just be certain that giving a handout in that moment is *the best way* to love your neighbor. Commitment to relationship—to truly loving a whole person, not just their need—is always harder than a one-time gift, yet it is to be desired, even when handing someone cash. So just be cautious.

Be aware of the dangers of handouts and try to choose a better alternative if possible, but also don't use "I don't give people money" as an excuse for not giving at all. As Anne Frank famously wrote, "No one has ever become poor by giving."

If you decide, as I have, not to give money to people unless you have a relationship with them—with the exception of when the Spirit directs otherwise—just decide where your money is going to go instead. Don't use it as a reason to stop giving. (I offer some practical advice about this in part four of this book.)

Jesus' statements about giving and debt must be guiding principles understood in light of His command to *truly* love people. We must use discernment when it comes to giving and debt. I believe we can honor Jesus' ideas about giving without providing someone with their last drink. I believe we can show people mercy by thoughtfully giving, while making the systems of giving more just. I believe there is a path forward that involves renewing life rather than disabling it.

JUSTICE, MERCY, AND THE ANGRY PROPHETS

"Do you prefer justice or mercy?" It was the only Myers-Briggs personality test question I hesitated on. I thought, "If I answer 'justice' (my knee-jerk reaction), I will have to consider myself apathetic. If I answer 'mercy,' I will feel more 'Christian.' If I were a lawyer, I would be a prosecuting attorney, but one who wishes he could defend people."

The question revealed something flawed about my theology—I viewed justice as something negative. For me, justice was the negative consequence of poor decisions. But, biblically speaking, justice is a positive concept—it means God making a wrong thing right. It isn't only about punishment, although that can be a component of it.

Likewise, the Myers-Briggs question made me realize that, today, justice is often cast as the negative side of mercy. But, biblically speaking, the two ideas complement one another: God is both just and merciful.

Yet what about the rest of us, who don't have perfect discernment, as God does—how can we balance justice and mercy in our lives? (I have found that the balance required is especially a struggle for people who work with those on the underside of power.)

How We Can Begin to Love Whole Communities

I believe we can bring justice *and* mercy to others. We can do so by looking at the whole person and all their concerns, including the injustices committed against them. We can help by bringing mercy and justice to communities, through the people present there already—working alongside them.

For example, instead of immediately springing into action, let's first stop to listen. Let's step back and evaluate the situation: What injustices are occurring? Where does mercy need to be offered? And how can we empower community leaders to correct injustices and offer compassionate (merciful) ministry?

There Is Tension Here—and That's Okay

There is no resolution to the tension between justice and mercy, but there are biblical ideas about how to love others with both justice and mercy. These ideas have changed the way I help the hurting in my community and how I engage in global development efforts.

The biblical prophets held mercy and justice in the balance. When they looked at the world, they saw that both of these elements must be present for God's love to be fully known—for His kingdom to arrive.

> "Wash! Make yourselves clean! Remove the evil of your doings from before my eyes! Cease to do evil! Learn to do good! Seek justice! Rescue the oppressed! Defend the orphan! Plead for the widow! Come now, and let us argue," says Yahweh. "Even though your sins are like scarlet, they will be white like snow; even though they are red like crimson, they shall become like wool."
>
> (Isaiah 1:16–18)

For justice to exist, purity must also exist. Unless we come to terms with God, it's difficult to come to terms with what we need to do for others.

At the core of empowering other people must be a deep spiritual awareness of ourselves. God desires for us to learn to do good and cease from doing evil. We must know Him deeply to be able to fully accomplish this. It's the epitome of the old adage, "You can't help someone else if you can't first help yourself," but with a twist: "You can't help someone else (bring them justice and mercy), if you don't first let God help you."

If forced to pinpoint the primary problem with both local and global development today, I would say, as I have said previously, that it is looking at the physical problems without looking at the spiritual issues, and looking at the spiritual problems without a concern for the physical issues.

Our efforts to empower others are often focused on either spiritual or physical poverty, when we really should focus on both. (See, for example, Micah 6:6–8; Amos 5:23–24.) Most of us have taken half of God's message to the world and left the other half.

God is a holistic community developer. He cares about the entire life of a person and the entire life of a community. God cares about their spiritual health *and* their physical health. The problem is that we don't, *really*, if we're honest with ourselves. *Truly* caring about another person often means giving of ourselves beyond the extent that we are comfortable. It often means facing issues in ourselves that we don't want to deal with. But, given the right motivation, we can change our apathy.

Feeling Pain like the Prophets Did

Once you meet people in deep and extreme poverty, you understand the fury of the prophets against injustice. It was in the slum in Bihar, India, where my heart cried out for justice and mercy.

"This part of the village needs clean water," the woman in her early forties remarked to my friend Biju Thomas, the director of Transformation India Movement (Jesus' Economy's partner in Bihar). She was grateful for the recent water well in her slum, but with thousands more living just down the road, she knew the people at the other end of the slum were still drinking dirty water. The look on her face as she expressed her slum's needs will never leave my mind. It was anger combined with pain—she was grateful for the recent success, but infuriated by the fact that everyone else with resources had abandoned her, outside of Transformation India Movement.

I felt the cry for justice rise in me again as another woman in a village said, "My baby is sick and has been for several weeks. I'm praying for him. He needs prayer." You could tell she was holding back the tears, and so was I.

"My baby's arm is broken—motorcycle accident," mentioned another woman in a different village. "He needs care," she said, "but I don't have any money."

For all three women, care was offered. Their stories, though, represent life in Bihar—and people all over the developing world, for that matter.

For many women in the developing world, help never comes. They are left in their suffering.

When women in Bihar find work, for example, it's hard labor—in the fields and at construction projects. And they still take care of their children and prepare all the food for their households each day. They handle nearly all matters for their families. They are strong, brave, and enduring. But they are still considered less than men.

Many women in developing economies lack opportunities that can change their economic situation. To address this, my friends in India are providing solutions that empower women.

"I have a sustainable job now. The women from my village come to me to have clothing made, for them and their children—and I can now make a living. My babies have the food they need," said a lady who had graduated from one of the Bridge of Hope Tailoring Centers that are provided by Transformation India Movement.

Only Jesus can offer this kind of empowerment to people all over the world. We have the opportunity to partner with Him to bring justice and mercy to the darkest situations.

But, amazingly, we continue to find excuses not to do so. One of the excuses I often hear involves "the problem with empowering women." The view is that the empowerment of women changes society too quickly and emasculates men. I asked my friend Biju, the leader of Transformation India Movement, about this. Specifically, I asked what the perception is of the empowered women in his culture.

He said the men are grateful because many of the women are doubling the incomes of their households. In addition, many of the men end up liking what Christians are doing so much—providing training for their spouses—that they end up coming to church.

Like the prophets, we should cry out for mercy and justice and then take action. These actions will be such a striking contrast to the apathy we see all around us that others will be astounded by them, as they were by the works of the Old Testament prophets and the early church apostles. Our world will know that when Jesus comes to town, it is good news for everyone.

WHEN JESUS COMES TO TOWN

Sounding a little surprised that I didn't understand why such a large crowd had come out that day, Biju said, "They came to be healed." Placing his hand on my shoulder, he then looked at me and declared, "When Jesus comes to town, people are healed."

With fervor and conviction in his tone, it was as if Biju was saying, "You—Mr. M.A. in Biblical Studies, who has edited a study Bible—do you actually know what the Bible says?"

You can live your entire life studying the Bible and not know what it actually means. Right there, in that moment, in Bihar, India, I realized that I knew the gospel but did not understand it.

It wasn't the first time I had seen people healed, but it had never dawned on me that healings are meant to be a major part of ministry—a major component of bringing justice and mercy to this world.

Freeing people not just from spiritual oppression, but also from physical oppression, is a central part of Jesus' message. Take a look at this passage from the beginning of Jesus' ministry. In the synagogue at Nazareth, He opens up an Isaiah scroll—at 61:1–2 and 58:6—and says:

> The Spirit of the Lord is upon me, because he has anointed me to proclaim good news to the poor. He has sent me to proclaim liberty to the captives and recovering of sight to the blind, to set at liberty those who are oppressed, to proclaim the year of the Lord's favor.
>
> (Luke 4:18–19 ESV)

Jesus, as the fulfillment of Scripture in Isaiah, chooses these lines to articulate what He is all about. He has come to proclaim "good news to the poor," which includes liberty for the captives and oppressed, and physical healing. The Greek word translated in Luke 4:18 as "good news" is the same word often translated as "the gospel." Jesus is saying that His gospel means freedom for the impoverished, marginalized, and oppressed. The gospel is about our salvation and it is about the physical transformation of our world.

It is *this message* that John the Baptist makes the way for. (See, for example, Mark 1:1–8.) And it is this message that ultimately confirms for John the Baptist who Jesus is. When Jesus is asked by John's disciples if He is indeed the one John has been waiting for, Jesus responds,

> Go and tell John what you have seen and heard: the blind receive sight, the lame walk, lepers are cleansed, the deaf hear; the dead are raised, the poor have good news announced to them.
>
> (Luke 7:22)

The gospel is all about Jesus coming to town and changing lives. It is about the blind seeing, the lame walking, the lepers being cleansed, the deaf hearing, the dead being raised, and the poor having good news announced to them.

Life transformation should be our expectation when spreading the good news about Jesus. Jesus is not just a message to be preached; through the Holy Spirit, He is at work in our very lives, healing and making broken beings whole again. Jesus is transforming lives here and now. The gospel unlocks the very power of God to change and transform humanity.

Think of all the times the gospel describes crowds surrounding Jesus and His disciples. (See, for example, Mark 3:7; Matthew 5:1; Luke 14:25.) And think of how this continues straight into the time of the apostles. (See, for example, Acts 2:5–41.) Why do we feel all that work has suddenly stopped?

There is no evidence in the early church, or in the Bible, that God has stopped performing miracles. There is no evidence that He has stopped speaking or that the gifts of the Spirit have ceased.

(See, for example, 1 Corinthians 12.) Those who preach such ideas are simply propagating myths. I believe that the performing of miracles should be going on right now, everywhere that the gospel is preached. Jesus, right now, wants to transform physical and spiritual lives. It is our unbelief that holds such things back from happening.

The blind deserve to see. The lame deserve to walk. The deaf deserve to hear. If people desire, they should have their demons cast out. Jesus wants to free people now. Let's bring the power of Christ to all who are impoverished—the spiritually and physically impoverished. When we pray, Jesus answers—in this life or the next. We will all be made whole again in Him.

The good news of Jesus *is* good news *for the poor*. When Jesus comes to town, people are healed. When Jesus comes to town, lives are renewed—restored—as they should be.

Our faith and our actions should be inseparable. Let's act like we actually believe in the Jesus of the Bible, for He is resurrected, alive, and working in powerful ways *today*.

I SAW JESUS ONCE

The large, concrete room in Bihar, India, was hot and humid. As drops of sweat clouded my eyes, I looked at Kari, who sat at a table on the other side of the room. Gracefully, she moved her hands across threads wound into newspaper clippings. The clippings were in the shapes of children's clothing. One by one, other women in the room were bringing clippings to Kari. My friend Biju leaned over and whispered to me, "She is testing them. She was once destitute, but through our empowering women program, she learned to be a seamstress and is now self-sustaining; she teaches these women to be the same."

Looking at Kari's eyes as she worked, I realized that this is what Jesus, the Carpenter, does. This is Jesus, working through her.

I Know Where Jesus Is and Will Be

Jesus says that when the world as we know it reaches its end, He will declare:

> "Come, you who are blessed by my Father, inherit the kingdom prepared for you from the foundation of the world. For I was hungry and you gave me food, I was thirsty and you gave me drink, I was a stranger and you welcomed me, I was naked and you clothed me, I was sick and you visited me, I was in prison and you came to me." Then the righteous will answer him, saying, "Lord, when did we see you hungry and feed you, or thirsty and give you drink? And when did we see you a stranger and welcome you, or naked

and clothe you? And when did we see you sick or in prison and visit you?" And the King will answer them, "Truly, I say to you, as you did it to one of the least of these my brothers, you did it to me."

(Matthew 25:34–40 ESV)

"Lord, when did we see you…?" "Here, here, and here," He essentially says, "among these people, everywhere. That's where I was and that's where I am." Jesus calls out to us, "I am the poor. I am the powerless. I am the marginalized. I am the imprisoned. I am the immigrant. I am the thirsty. I am the hungry. I am."

"I am" (Exodus 3:14), God said to Moses, when describing Himself. Inherent in his self-description are the questions, "Who am I? Where am I?"

The King Jesus answers, "I am in them, working. Through my Spirit, I am there, among those who are cast aside by society." "As you did it to one of the least of these…, you did it to me." In other words, "When you receive them, you receive Me."

I'm not sure about you, but when Jesus comes to earth again, I want to be found with the impoverished. Because, as I understand it, that's where Jesus is. Kari knows this and lives it. Kari sees Jesus every day. And when I see Kari, I see Jesus.

The God of Colors and Curry

Kari showed me each of the beautiful creations of these wonderful women, one by one. The colors were as bright as India, the threading as delicate as the balance of a good curry. In the colors, I saw beauty and hope. I saw Jesus turning craft into livelihood, and livelihood into freedom. *Here He is—where am I?*

I already knew that I wanted to empower women in Bihar. I desired to help them take their craft to the next level, so they could sell products on the Western market, generating more income for their families and communities. I had been given the vision of the nonprofit Jesus' Economy. It was my job to be faithful to its ideas, including connecting entrepreneurs in the developing world to global commerce. But I didn't really know what that vision meant until that moment.

In fact, in that moment, I wondered if I really knew Jesus at all. Because looking at the way Kari represented the great Carpenter, I wondered if I would ever represent Him as well as she did. In the colors and the smell of curry, I saw hope not just for these women, but for my own heart.

As I looked at Kari, I thought of Mary the mother of Jesus. Mary's response to God was simple:

> Behold, I am the servant of the Lord; let it be to me according to your word.   (Luke 1:38 ESV)

Kari has this type of obedience to Jesus. She has chosen not just to rise out of poverty, but also to help others do the same. She knows what it means to share the heart of God. She could capitalize on her skills and monopolize them, but instead she teaches her skills to others, because that's what Jesus would do.

When I examine Mary's heart against my own, I know that my heart is lacking. It's selfish and ugly; there is much growth yet to happen. My heart is not like Mary's, nor is my heart like Kari's.

I had just traveled a dusty road in Bihar, but when I looked into the eyes of Kari, I saw beauty. I imagined what could be if Bihar were renewed. I saw in my mind's eye a vision of streams of water flowing, making beauty out of the dust. I saw God renewing this land, as a sign of the new creation to come. God is making beautiful things, in the colors and the curry, and among the impoverished.

I saw Jesus once. Do you see Him?

TRUE RELIGION IS THIS

Faith and actions are inseparable. The New Testament writer James ties this issue directly into how we should approach and understand poverty:

> My brothers, do not hold your faith in our glorious Lord Jesus Christ with partiality. For if someone enters into your assembly in fine clothing with a gold ring on his finger, and a poor person in filthy clothing also enters, and you look favorably on the one wearing the fine clothing and you say, "Be seated here in a good place," and to the poor person you say, "You stand or be seated there by my footstool," have you not made distinctions among yourselves and become judges with evil thoughts? (James 2:1–4)

It is always easier to be friends with someone like you—someone you approve of. If we're really honest with ourselves, most of us want to befriend the *most* powerful person in the room, not the *least* powerful. Such a response may seem obvious, but think on it for a moment. What are the ramifications if we act on this tendency?

The inclination to favor one person over another reveals something about our view of God, others, and faith. When we show partiality to the wealthy person over the impoverished person, to the loved over the unloved, to the popular over the outcast, we betray a part of our very faith—impartial love for others. (See, for example, Matthew 22:37–40.)

Our partiality crops up in many settings—from how we treat someone who walks into our church, to who we are willing to have a discussion with at a coffee shop, to our preference on business trips to set up meetings with the wealthy instead of the impoverished.

Is This Fundraising Version of Me Still Me?

On a fundraising trip for Jesus' Economy, I was really upset about how little giving I had seen from some very wealthy people. I was excited that we had broken even and that we had been well received by an incredible congregation on our first day there, but we were well short of my financial goal for the trip.

I began to imagine how I could turn the trip around—generating the funds we needed. I discussed this with Kalene, my wife, who was on the trip with me. (A good wife is also a good conscience, and my wife is always there to keep my ego, and motives, in check.) Kalene said to me, "Have you prayed about your feelings? I worry that your thoughts are so much on the money that you're losing sight of what God is doing—or wants to do." I was offended, but not angry—I mean, come on, I was raising money for the impoverished in Bihar, India. How wrong could my motives be?

But my motives *were* wrong—Kalene was right. She encouraged me to pray about it. I confessed my sin to God, confirming to Him that He had told me to come on this trip and expressing that I was confused about why there wasn't more funding coming in. God promptly said to me, "I did call you here but not for the reasons you think."

And that's when I began looking for the reasons why He *had* called me to go on this trip. Before I knew it, I had a wonderful time with a local Bible college. The worshipful actions of the students in chapel called me to a higher version of worshipfulness. Their self-sacrificial way of living made me realize (as I often do) that I had more to learn than to teach. I also realized that, at the very least, it was for these young people that God had called me on this trip. He had called me to share the wisdom He had taught me, but He had also called me to come and learn from these wonderful young believers—living on fire for Jesus as bi-vocational ministers, mainly from poverty. It was likely this roomful of young people—not the wealthy I had been spending much of my time with—who would transform the world.

"It is easier for a camel to go through the eye of a needle than a rich person into the kingdom of God" (Matthew 19:24) rang in my ears, as well as "Blessed are you who are poor, for yours is the kingdom of God" (Luke 6:20). Jesus spent most of His ministry with the impoverished. And history tells us that it is the impoverished who are most likely to respond to the gospel. There is something about poverty that often makes people aware of their status before God. Perhaps it is that physical poverty, and the reliance on God it brings, makes a person more likely to realize their need for God. The impoverished often welcome Jesus with open arms, while the wealthy and self-reliant often turn away.

God checked my heart in this moment. I quickly realized, as I would also preach that day, that it wasn't my job to be everything to all people. It wasn't my job to make everything happen—or even to be successful in fundraising. It was my job to be everything to the person in front of me. And I knew exactly who I had to be everything to in that moment—these young people. I needed them as much as they needed me. Our first language was different—theirs was Spanish—and our background was different, but Jesus was the same. Jesus was everything to all of us.

God has called us to love others without partiality. He has called us to look at others and do for them as we would want them to do for us—aside from how they appear or what they have to offer in return. Did these young people have fiscal support to offer me? No. But the spiritual support they offered me—and the chance to witness their love of Jesus in worship—was a gift worth more than all the money in the world. (Kalene and I regularly say that, even all these years later, our time with that group was one of the most impactful ministry experiences of our lives.)

I am sure you already know all this to be true, but are you practicing it today? Really, take a moment and think about it: Are you loving others without partiality? And if not, how can you change your behavior? How can you change the particular thoughts that led to that negative behavior?

Imagine how incredibly different, and better, the world would be if we loved others equally. Think about what it would show to the world about Jesus and His love for *all* of us.

Everything Is Reversed in God's Kingdom

> Did not God choose the poor of the world to be rich in faith, and
> heirs of the kingdom that he has promised to those who love him?
> But you have dishonored the poor!… If you carry out the royal law
> according to the scripture, "You shall love your neighbor as your-
> self," you are doing well. But if you show partiality, you commit
> sin, and thus are convicted by the law as transgressors. For whoev-
> er keeps the whole law but stumbles in one point only has become
> guilty of all of it.   (James 2:5–6, 8–10)

The impoverished of the world are chosen to be rich in faith. In God's
kingdom, things are reversed. You would expect James to tell us that those
who are rich are surely blessed, and thus are clearly the most thankful (and
perhaps, by extension, inheritors of great things), but he doesn't. Instead, he
tells us that the poor are rich in faith, and thus heirs of a great blessing—
God's kingdom.

James then goes on to confront us about that which we so easily forget:
We're called to *really* love our neighbor, as we would want to be loved; and
that means (again) avoiding partiality. When we show partiality, we not
only do wrong by others, but we actually go against what James calls the
"royal law" of God.

When we stumble on the point of showing partiality, we are breaking a
fundamental value of the entire law of God: loving Him and other people.
We cannot show our love for Him without showing our love for others. We
cannot love as He does without loving all people. Thankfully, God is always
quick to show mercy and grace, but this does not make our wrongdoings
against others acceptable or easily excusable.

When reading James' thoughts, I am struck by the fact that he presents
us not just with a commandment, but also with an opportunity. Here, in this
little New Testament letter, it is revealed to us how God's kingdom works.
We're given a chance to turn away from what we think will fulfill us and
turn toward the fulfilling work of God. We're given a chance to show true
love for the inheritors of God's kingdom, the impoverished. Here in James,
we're shown—as we also are in Matthew—that we're all impoverished in

some way. The apostle Matthew perhaps summarizes this idea best when he quotes Jesus as saying, "Blessed are the poor in spirit, because theirs is the kingdom of heaven" (Matthew 5:3).

And that brings us to an incredible truth about God's kingdom. Those of us with wealth will often find that the impoverished will teach us about truly loving Jesus. And those of us without wealth will find that the wealthy can offer empowerment—leading to the overcoming of physical poverty itself. And we will all find that we're in equal need of the Savior, Jesus.

James offers us a powerful opportunity and an incredible message—whether we're wealthy or not. In God's kingdom, the only difference between those who are wealthy and those who are not is the ease by which they enter His kingdom and join His work. And if God's kingdom is all about self-sacrificially loving Jesus, then those of us who are wealthy have a great deal to learn. I think that starts with our view of money, because it will reveal where our heart is.

ANJALI AND REDEEMING CASH MONEY

For years, she had been chanting to the gods. From a remote village in the developing world, Anjali had walked miles to school in over 100-degree weather, often with more than 75 percent humidity, and the teacher didn't even show up most of the time. This was life for her.

Anjali's father was an addict. Her mother, Amita, was just trying to hold her family together. Over time, the love of Christians in their community—shown through tangible actions to alleviate poverty—brought Amita to Jesus, the prophet from Israel, who had risen from the dead and who promised equality and offered hope.

The family's money was running out. Anjali's father was spending his earnings to feed his addiction instead of his family. Anjali's mother realized she would have to get a job in the city for her family to survive. So she decided to move to the city—to work for my friend's ministry, as a cook at an orphanage. Anjali's younger brother went, too, and lived in the boys' orphanage, but Anjali wanted to stay; she wasn't sure what she thought of her mother's new religion. Finally, after she realized that she would die if she stayed with her father, she caught a bus to the city.

Anjali was too old to live in the girls' orphanage—she was sixteen—so my friend arranged for her to live with his family. He told her that if she would do some housework and cooking, his wife would mentor her in order to get her ready for private school. (She was very far behind because of the poor education she had been receiving.) Also, in return for her work, she would have her room and board covered. She would become part of the family but be within three minutes' walking distance of her mother and brother.

Anjali had thought she would continue chanting to her gods, but she physically could no longer do so. The power of the Holy Spirit in my friend's household kept her from speaking to them. It was a miracle, but it felt oppressive to her. She was sad and depressed when I first met her—I didn't see a single smile on her face for nearly a week.

And then it happened: At a youth seminar about Jesus, she decided to become a Christian, citing her lack of ability to chant to her gods as Jesus' power over them. She also cited the incredible love she had been shown by my friend's family. As Anjali walked forward to be prayed for, I saw a smile on her face from ear to ear. It was one of the most beautiful things I have ever seen.

That evening, she said to my friend's wife, "I understand that Christians hear God talking to them." She asked how she could hear Him too. She was told to start reading her Bible and praying, which is what I saw her doing for more hours each day than nearly any Christian I have ever met. She fell in love with Jesus because of the love that had been shown to her by Christians—who loved her completely and wholly.

Every time I tell this story, people smile. But as soon as I start talking about money—and how God's view of money made all this happen—they get a little uncomfortable. I see hands cover wallets.

Money matters: it has the power to change lives. Money can create jobs, start a church, or meet basic needs. Money is what makes it possible for people like Anjali to experience Jesus.

There is fiscal intelligence in many developing-world churches, just as there was in the early church. The following examples from the lives of early Christian leaders provide some principles for redeeming cash.

Saint Peter Wants to Redistribute Assets

Talking about wealth distribution generally infuriates people, at least in my particular Western context. If you bring up wealth redistribution, communism and socialism are almost immediately mentioned to combat the idea. The only sermon that can make a Western churchgoer more uncomfortable than one about tithing—giving at least ten percent of your income to the church or other select Christian causes—is wealth redistribution. Yet, if we're honest with ourselves, we will acknowledge that is exactly what the earliest Christians practiced:

> And [the early Christians] were devoting themselves to the teaching of the apostles and to fellowship [spending time together], to the breaking of bread [the practice of communion] and to prayers. And fear came on every soul, and many wonders and signs [miracles] were being performed by the apostles. And all who believed were in the same place, and had everything in common [meaning that they shared their assets]. And they began selling their possessions and property, and distributing these things to all, to the degree that anyone had need. And every day, devoting themselves to meeting with one purpose in the temple courts [the Jewish temple in Jerusalem] and breaking bread from house to house, they were eating their food with joy and simplicity of heart, praising God and having favor with all the people. And the Lord was adding every day to the total of those who were being saved.
>
> (Acts 2:42–47)

It's understandable that the idea of wealth redistribution makes capitalists uncomfortable. They believe the market should dictate the winners and the losers. And generally, that works in business—up until it ignores the impoverished (the Anjalis of the world). Capitalism works—up until it means the rich get richer while the poor get poorer.

That said, there are some important things to understand about the early church. The New Testament church was not a government, and a pope out of Rome did not lead it. Instead, the early believers were caring individuals who gave up everything for the betterment of others "to the degree that anyone had need." They did so because they believed that people should not suffer. In addition, they believed that what ultimately mattered was Jesus—more than anything this world could offer—and thus viewed their process of empowering others as part of the process of Christ transforming the world.

I am not advocating socialism—and by no means am I suggesting a communistic framework. I am suggesting, as I often put it, that we all "give to the point it hurts a little," and that we all give to the point that poverty can be sustainably alleviated. And I am suggesting that the church be the center of this work.

As C. S. Lewis wrote in *Mere Christianity*, "I do not believe one can settle how much we ought to give. I am afraid the only safe rule is to give more than we can spare." In other words, give to the point it hurts.

The Radical Early Church

The views of the early church may seem completely radical, but when thought about in terms of the eternality of God's work, they're really not. If we're all on the way to dying—and the giving up of what we don't need in order to help someone else can better their life, or even save it—the early Christians' values are actually reasonable.

What do "things" matter in terms of eternity? What good does a new luxury item do me when I'm dead? However, if selling my possessions—or giving up that extra money in my bank account—can grant someone else life, suddenly my decision to give becomes the most important thing I can do.

It is very difficult to live the fullness of life in Christ while on this earth if the basics of life are a complete struggle. By giving from our excess to others, we create the balance necessary for others to do the work Christ has for them.

Many Western Christians consider the natural workings of capitalism to be the answer to all economic problems, including poverty. But this view can become an excuse to not help the impoverished, a number of whom face issues beyond their control—issues that ultimately hinder their efforts at starting and maintaining their own businesses.

If we don't give freely to empower others, we lose sight of what it means to be Christian. Of course, I mean this within the context of giving with discernment, as anyone has need. (For, as my friends who work in areas that have masses of dollars poured into them—like Haiti—can attest, the results can be tragic if we're not careful.)

Another Great Divorce

Currently, giving to the impoverished and giving to the ministries in the church are divided: ministries to the impoverished are one thing and ministries to the "regular" church members, such as programming or education, are another. Such a division cannot be found in the early church—work with the impoverished was part of what the church did. They weren't interested in money for better programs or services.

The effects of this problem are dire: the church has excess money—clearly enough to buy giant buildings and state-of-the-art, surround-sound systems—whereas there isn't enough money among ministries to the impoverished to go around. Nonprofits are constantly fundraising to meet their needs.

Giving in the church has also become limited in scope to merely "my 10 percent," which does not appear to even be an option on Jesus' radar. Take, for example, Jesus telling the rich young man to sell everything and follow Him (Matthew 19:16–22) or His comment that the woman who contributed two small coins had given more than all others had from their excess (Mark 12:41–44). When Jesus talks about following Him, He isn't asking people to attend church services and give 10 percent: He is asking for everything—complete and utter dedication.

We wouldn't even have a problem with wealth redistribution if it was contextualized within a just and merciful church, in which we see where the money goes. We only dislike it because of the exploitation we have seen of it. Christians from the Western world generally hate the "tax man" because we're all aware that the government does not make the best use of the money it mandates from us, but we make little effort to provide a substitute. Our governments are involved in welfare programs because the church has failed to meet its obligations to the most needy. Thus, wealth redistribution at the governmental level—which happens in democracies, too, not just socialist or communistic societies—exists because Christians have failed to carry out a large part of Jesus' mission. While we were busy building large facilities, and in doing so looking like just another entertainment venue, the government had to help the people we weren't.

Today, if the church's mission to make more disciples of Jesus were unified with our mission to help those living in poverty, we would no longer see a separation between giving to the impoverished and giving to the church—it would all be the same to us. We would understand that the primary intent of our giving is to help the impoverished, and thus we would have even more desire to give. Giving isn't a burden when you see the lives that it changes.

Reclaiming the church's rightful work is what creating a new economy of self-sacrifice is all about.

Helping the Impoverished with Our Actions and Money

Note that, from nearly the beginning of the church, there have been problems associated with helping those in need. The early church's actions illustrate for us that "giving freely" needs to come from a holistic framework:

As [Jesus'] disciples were increasing in number, a complaint arose by the Greek-speaking Jews against the Hebraic Jews because their widows were being overlooked in the daily distribution of food. So the twelve summoned the community of disciples and said, "It is not desirable that we neglect the word of God to serve tables. So, brothers, select from among you seven men of good reputation, full of the Spirit and wisdom, whom we will put in charge of this need. But we will devote ourselves to prayer and to the ministry of the word." And the statement pleased the whole group, and they chose [seven men], whom they stood before the apostles. And they prayed and placed their hands on them. And the word of God kept spreading, and the number of disciples in Jerusalem was increasing greatly.   (Acts 6:1–7)

Helping those in need is not simple, and apparently never has been. The early church overcame their cultural (and racial) divisions, and consequent wealth distribution problems, by focusing on leadership. The apostles looked at the strengths among themselves and saw that they weren't capable of handling the issues at stake while continuing their other work. It wasn't that the issue of helping the impoverished was unimportant to the apostles; it's that it was so important that if they failed to address it adequately, they would be failing their mission in general. Failure in one area of their ministry equaled failure in another. Their ministry to the impoverished was directly connected to their ministry to spread the gospel.

When faced with the major issue of how to best help the impoverished in their community, the apostles addressed this problem by appointing good leadership to oversee the ongoing efforts. This does not mean a dismissal of the poor, but an elevation of the poor.

Notice how the apostles decided to come alongside the widows, to actually care for their problems. Also notice how the leaders were appointed to assess the needs and solve the problems—and how they were leaders from the community itself. This is what we call asset-based community development: assessing the assets *and* the needs of a community and empowering local leaders to use those assets to overcome the poverty that is present, thereby restoring and renewing life as it should be.

But Let's Be Sure We *Really* Overcome Poverty

The early church ensured that poverty was overcome in a healthy and productive way. We see this in Paul's ministry, when he tells Timothy:

> Honor widows who are truly widows. But if any widow has children or grandchildren, they must learn to show profound respect for their own household first, and to pay back recompense to their parents, for this is pleasing in the sight of God. But the widow who is one truly, and is left alone, has put her hope in God and continues in her petitions and prayers night and day. But the one who lives for sensual pleasure is dead even though she lives. And command these things, in order that they may be irreproachable. But if someone does not provide for his own relatives, and especially the members of his household, he has denied the faith and is worse than an unbeliever. (1 Timothy 5:3–8)

Notice that Paul tells Timothy to confirm that the widows are indeed widows in need. (Widows would have been some of the most impoverished people in the first-century AD, since men were the only ones capable of earning a regular income.)

Paul creates a provision for ensuring that people who seek help are actually impoverished—there's a lesson there for us. He even notes that a widow's family should be the first to care for her, and that Timothy should be teaching his congregation this.

Paul then tells Timothy to be sure that the women he is empowering are actually impoverished because of real need. He makes a provision for ruling someone out who is making poor lifestyle choices. This is bold, but sometimes necessary. Again, it comes back to the question, "Is money what this person *really* needs? Or are the issues deeper than that?"

I don't think that Paul's remark about a widow's devotion to God should be taken as his suggesting that we shouldn't help non-believers; instead, I think Paul is simply tying in the gospel to poverty alleviation, because he sees the power of its work in our lives. I believe this to be the case because Paul, like the other New Testament writers, lived by the principle of loving all people in tangible ways. We see this through his actions in the book of Acts and his own letters.

Notice that, for Paul, all of this is a command that Timothy is meant to carry out. Paul is serious about the ways poverty is alleviated. He goes on to say:

> Let a widow be put on the list if she is not less than sixty years old, the wife of one husband, being well-attested by good works, if she has brought up children, if she has shown hospitality, if she has washed the feet of the saints, if she has helped those who are oppressed, if she has devoted herself to every good work.
>
> (1 Timothy 5:9–10)

Paul does not mean that women under sixty should be ruled out—instead, he is claiming a provision for women under sixty to be included. It seems that behind the scenes here is Paul's view that women under sixty who are widows can likely provide for themselves. But Paul still allows for a clause that can alleviate the poverty of those who are serving the church and likely have serious needs (they have children to provide for).

For Paul, the only way to confirm that these women seriously need the church's help is if the leaders of the church have seen the fruits of the Spirit in their lives. He wants to see that the financial support will also have an impact on the community, that it will be well used. Paul gets even more strict (and shocking) with his standards:

> But refuse younger widows, for whenever their physical desires lead them away from Christ, they want to marry, thus incurring condemnation because they have broken their former pledge. And at the same time also, going around from house to house, they learn to be idle, and not only idle, but also gossipy and busybodies, saying the things that are not necessary. Therefore I want younger widows to marry, to bear children, to manage a household, to give the adversary no opportunity for reproach. For already some have turned away and followed after Satan. If any believing woman has widows, she must help them, and the church must not be burdened, in order that it may help those who are truly widows.
>
> (1 Timothy 5:11–16)

In Paul's framework, behind these statements is his view on vows of celibacy. He is warding off the possibility of certain women among Timothy's community taking a false or unadvised vow of celibacy and devotion to the church, just to break it when they can go back to married life. Paul thus encourages younger women not to seek some false piety by choosing celibacy after being widowed—instead, they should be free to marry again. He is chiefly concerned with people becoming incorrectly dependent on the church, and eventually a burden to it, through idle behavior. He says all this with the provision that young widows are certainly allowed to continue on as widows, but that it won't be the church's responsibility to care for them.

Despite appearances, Paul is not making some sexist statement here—he is actually trying to prevent a problem he has noticed occurring. He doesn't mention men in this instance because men, no matter their age, would have been expected to work in his society. (That was their only means of support, because only widows were fully supported by the church.) Paul sets up provisions for overcoming poverty without offering support that will ultimately hurt those being served and the church. As such, his principles could actually be applied to people today.

If someone can care for themselves, the church should be there to empower them to do so. If someone cannot care for themselves, the church should be willing to support them. And for each person asking for assistance, we should be sure that they actually need it. By not living by this rule, we open up the possibility for idleness to lead to evil ruling over someone's life, and for our churches to be burdened in the process.

This makes me again think of Anjali. My friend didn't offer her a free ride. He offered her empowerment (a place to live *and* work), and it led to her accepting Jesus. As a result, she will probably lead others to Jesus and empowerment in Him. But giving doesn't always work this way.

The Problems with Givers

Giving in the early church was self-sacrificial and incredible:

> Now the group of those who believed [in Jesus] were one heart and soul, and no one said anything of what belonged to him was his own, but all things were theirs in common. And with great power the apostles were giving testimony to the resurrection of the Lord Jesus, and great grace was on them all. For there was not even anyone needy among them, because all those who were owners of plots of land or houses were selling them and bringing the proceeds of the things that were sold and placing them at the feet of the apostles. And it was being distributed to each as anyone had need. So Joseph, who was called Barnabas by the apostles (which is translated "son of encouragement"), a Levite of Cyprus by nationality, sold a field that belonged to him and brought the money and placed it at the feet of the apostles. (Acts 4:32–37)

A world where people are this generous seems fictional. But it could happen again. If we were all to give of ourselves for others, the world would look entirely different.

I often wonder how different the demonstration of the mission of Christ in the world would be if His followers obeyed Him by giving—if all of us Christians were actually willing to empower others, no matter what it cost us. I think being a Christian would become a nearly irresistible idea—like it was for Anjali.

But it's certainly not all roses. A brief glimpse into the dark events following these incredible times in the early church demonstrates this:

> Now...Ananias, together with his wife Sapphira, sold a piece of property, and he kept back for himself some of the proceeds, and his wife was aware of it. And he brought a certain part and placed it at the feet of the apostles. But Peter said, "Ananias, for what reason has Satan filled your heart, that you lied to the Holy Spirit and kept back for yourself some of the proceeds of the piece of land? When it remained to you, did it not remain yours? And when it was sold, was it at your disposal? How is it that you have contrived this deed in your heart? You have not lied to people, but to God!" And when Ananias heard these words, he fell down and died. And great fear came on all those who heard about it.... [After] about three hours,...his wife came in, not knowing what had happened. And Peter said to her, "Tell me whether you both were paid this much for the piece of land." And she said, "Yes, this much." So Peter said to her, "How is it that it was agreed by you two to test the Spirit of the Lord? Behold, the feet of those who buried your husband are at the door, and they will carry you out!" And immediately she fell down at his feet and died.... And great fear came on the whole church and on all who heard about these things.
>
> (Acts 5:1–5, 7–11)

Ananias and Sapphira were giving because it felt good and it looked good. They didn't seem to be interested in the actual result. Thus, there was no toleration from God.

The early church never requested that Ananias and Sapphira give everything they had. They didn't even ask them to sell their property; instead, Ananias and Sapphira chose to give. Also, for no reason outside of wanting to look good, they chose to be deceptive when doing so.

The story of Ananias and Sapphira, for all its complexity, really comes back to a simple lesson: God desires every part of us, but He desires our hearts (the proverbial birthplace of our intentions) the most. When we give, it must be honoring to Him and others, and it must be done in a fashion that is honest. We should never give for any reason other than wanting to experience the joy of being obedient to Jesus.

Paul Desires Money for the Impoverished Church

Paul regularly makes his own living—by being a tentmaker—yet he is also not bashful about simply collecting money for an impoverished church: "But now I am traveling to Jerusalem, serving the saints. For Macedonia and Achaia were pleased to make some contribution for the poor among the saints in Jerusalem" (Romans 15:25–26).

The Jerusalem church, which is where the church began, couldn't provide for all the needs of their community. Paul was hardly involved in the Jerusalem church and had nothing to do with its founding or ongoing ministry, but he made sure that they were taken care of.

When we approach ministry for Jesus, we must look at the world the same way: there are some people who can be simply empowered—after which they will be good to go, maybe even without funding—and there are other people who will likely always need help. (This is why Jesus' Economy offers grants to churches, but microloans to businesses.)

Churches should be self-sustaining whenever possible, and I think this should always be our expectation, but it's important to remember that churches face problems that businesses do not—especially churches serving primarily impoverished communities. Some churches may never be able to make it on their own. If that's the case, and it's legitimate, we should be there to bless them.

On the opposite side, if a church becomes wealthy someday, it should contribute toward providing grants for other churches.

The early church's system was to give freely and as anyone had need. But they also distributed assistance—and empowerment—with serious thought and prayer. Likewise, we should honor Jesus' teachings on giving, while also honoring His commandment to love our neighbor, by considering all the effects of our actions upon our neighbor.

Knowing When Not to Take a Paycheck

Similar to how there is a time to just give a grant and a time to provide a microloan, there is also a time for pastors to take a salary and a time for them not to. For example, in Bihar, India, it's critical for pastors to not ask anything of communities when entering them, because that's what priests from other religions do. That is why it's a good thing for these pastors to have grant money to fund them for a while. In other regions, it's important that pastors not receive money from outside sources at all, because then people become suspicious of their motivations—is this just a job for them?

I had the blessing of the no-paycheck model for a while. The money that established Jesus' Economy at its founding was all from Kalene and me, with none coming back out to us. We and the rest of the staff were all volunteer laborers in the mission. I wanted the charity to begin with a clear and decisive action that demonstrated, "Kalene and I will always give first before asking of you."

It wasn't necessarily my intention for Jesus' Economy to begin this way, or the intention of the others on our team to give so much of their time without getting anything tangible in return, but God provided us with the opportunity. And that's how we viewed it—the burden was light because it was Jesus' work in our lives.

That doesn't mean it wasn't difficult or even painful. It certainly wasn't fun for me to leave my job to go full-time with Jesus' Economy. I did so without the promise of a paycheck, and I watched friends and colleagues distance themselves from me. My lifestyle choices made people uncomfortable. Or perhaps it was that I no longer had power; I could no longer make other people's publishing dreams come true.

But when you're focusing on God's efforts in the world, you have a supreme confidence in where things are going. The moment may be hard, but you know the trajectory. You're aware that the faith you have will make the hopes you have for the lives of others realized. I've seen this to be true in my own life. This is also the biblical worldview—perhaps even the common ministry practice of the early church.

Paul lived without a paycheck for a while, for strategic reasons:

> Do we not have the right to eat and drink?... Or do only I and Barnabas not have the right to refrain from working? Who ever serves as a soldier at his own expense? Who plants a vineyard and does not eat the fruit of it? Who shepherds a flock and does not drink from the milk of the flock?... If we have sown spiritual things among you, is it too great a thing if we reap material things from you? If others share this right over you, do we not do so even more? Yet we have not made use of this right, but we endure all things, in order that we may not cause any hindrance to the gospel of Christ.
> (1 Corinthians 9:4, 6–7, 11–12)

Paul and Barnabas should have been able to receive Corinthian support for their ministry at any time, but they did not demand this; instead, they set themselves up to be above reproach. Paul goes on to make this point even more drastically:

> For if I proclaim the gospel, it is not to me a reason for boasting, for necessity is imposed on me. For woe is to me if I do not proclaim the gospel. For if I do this voluntarily, I have a reward, but if I do so unwillingly, I have been entrusted with a stewardship. What then is my reward? That when I proclaim the gospel, I may offer the gospel free of charge, in order not to make full use of my right in the gospel.   (1 Corinthians 9:16–18)

And with that, Paul indicates that the reward of all of our efforts for God is the proclamation that Jesus lives and saves. If our focus is not upon that, then what is the point of our giving our time and money?

But note that Paul is *not* saying that it is wrong for him to receive a paycheck. In fact, he is saying the opposite: he has every right to do so. Paul elsewhere says, "'You shall not muzzle an ox while it is treading out the grain,' and, 'The laborer deserves to be paid'" (1 Timothy 5:18 NRSV). The apostle is referencing Deuteronomy 25:4, and Deuteronomy 24:15 and Leviticus 19:13, respectively. In the reference to paying the laborer, Paul applies the same principle from the Old Testament Scriptures that

Jesus Himself applied. Jesus used this principle to make the point that His followers should go out on the mission in faith, without being overly concerned for provisions, but that they should also receive the payment for their work that is provided. (See Matthew 10:10; Luke 10:7.)

It is not more righteous to go without a paycheck. And when it comes to supporting the ministry work of others, we should go out of our way to make sure that they are well taken care of. This was exactly Paul's expectation of the Corinthians and of the Ephesians whom he addressed in 1 Timothy. Likewise, Jesus expected people to take care of the missionaries He was sending out.

When it comes to being a pioneering missionary yourself, just be aware that God may ask you to do what Paul did with the Corinthians—to make the self-sacrificial play. God may ask you to go out on faith alone. God may ask you to serve a people group while being bi-vocational. God may ask you to start a ministry without knowing where it will go or whether people will initially support it.

We cannot define success monetarily. Financial support for a ministry does not validate it. What really matters is whether *you* are faithful to what God has asked you to do and trust in His provision.

The idea is that we should rely on faith, but always be open to being paid for the faithful work. Self-sacrifice is the economy, but the love of the economy of Jesus may come back to us in the form of payment, food, shelter, or other provisions.

Everything that Paul and other the early believers did with their money and time was for the purpose of making Jesus known. It was for the Anjalis of the world. The efforts of the early Christians were founded in love, from the redistribution of assets to the sacrificing of themselves so that the work of God could be made known. There wasn't fear in their work—there was dedication. If we, as Christians today, could have the same kind of faith and love, the world would be different indeed. May our actions say as much about our faith as our words do.

SAINT PAUL SAYS LITTLE (YET IMPLIES A LOT) ABOUT POVERTY

What a person really thinks about poverty is articulated most clearly by how they live. Similarly, what someone really thinks about the good news of Jesus is perhaps best shown by the sacrifices and seemingly drastic life changes they make for Jesus.

Jesus may never ask you to do the things other Christians have done in the past. He may never ask you to sell your home or give all your stuff away. He may never ask you to literally lay down your life for another person. But if we are honest with ourselves, there are *many* things that we hope Jesus won't ask us to give up or do. We might even become angry or resentful at even the thought of the sacrifice.

Yet, we can be sure that anything that interferes with our authentic relationship with Jesus will be something He will ask us to reevaluate, no matter what it is.

The missing part of the gospel for many Americans is self-sacrifice. We've gladly embraced Jesus' love without acknowledging what it cost Him to give it. The love of God should prompt us to respond in love. The thought that there are people in the world who have yet to hear of salvation in Jesus should prompt us to do everything in our power to share this message.

Our hearts should be begging God to reveal how we can thank Him for creation and salvation. We don't do this mindlessly, or out of coercion, but because of the great love God has shown us.

When it comes to living Jesus' economy, the economy of self-sacrifice, I come back to the same thought over and over again. Am I doing all I can to live the currency of love? Am I doing my best to demonstrate by my actions the thankfulness I have for Christ? Am I *living love*, self-sacrificially?

This is how I define love: self-sacrifice for the betterment of another. That's how Jesus defined love: "No one has greater love than this, to lay down one's life for one's friends" (John 15:13 NRSV).

Whatever God Asks, We Must Do

When the early church addressed the matter of poverty and missions, their first questions were not, "How can we get *them*, those people over there, to change their ways?" or "How can I convince people to give?" The questions were, "*How can I* change my ways?" and "What am I willing to give?" Their example, how they lived self-sacrificially for Jesus, became the model that encouraged others to give.

The early church missionary Paul and his colleague Sosthenes were unafraid and unashamed when dealing with poverty and spreading the good news of Jesus. They were willing to do *whatever it took* to spread Jesus' gospel to people around the world. Paul and Sosthenes were willing to be poor, and even homeless, for the sake of Jesus. In a letter to the Corinthian church, Paul expresses:

> Until the present hour we are both hungry and thirsty and poorly clothed and roughly treated and homeless, and we toil, working with our own hands. When we are reviled, we bless; when we are persecuted, we endure; when we are slandered, we encourage. We have become like the refuse of the world, the offscouring of all things, until now. (1 Corinthians 4:11–13)

When I read passages like this, I am struck by the differences between how Paul lived and how I live—I am brought to the realization that my heart still has a long way to go in fully understanding, and living for, Jesus.

Later, in another letter to the Corinthians, Paul notes that he may be sorrowful, but he is also rejoicing, because although he is poor, he is making many people rich—spiritually rich—through sharing the saving message of Jesus. Paul goes on to say that he may have nothing, but he actually possesses everything: he possesses salvation and the Holy Spirit through Jesus. (See 2 Corinthians 6:10.)

So what did Paul really think of the impoverished and the way poverty should be approached? Paul respected the impoverished, all the way to the point of being willing to be like them. Before becoming a Christian, he had wealth, but he sacrificed it for Christ—he did whatever Jesus asked of him.

Paul didn't see a difference between himself and those living in poverty—they were one and the same. His concern was the good news of Jesus, who came as Savior to die and rise for humanity. For Paul, living among the poor (sometimes as a poor person), was often how he spread the good news. Whatever Christ asked of Paul, he was willing to do.

Even though Paul lived the gospel—to the point of living in poverty and having violence committed against him—he says surprisingly little about the impoverished. This could lead us to believe that caring for the impoverished was unimportant to him, but it seems more likely that he says so little about the impoverished because it was a given to him that believers in Christ would help others. The focus of Paul's letters, then, becomes the things he considers less likely to be the focus of the communities he is serving.

Saint Paul continues to shock me, even after all these years. There are days when I feel as if I am reading his letters for the first time. I believe this is because, ever since I gave my life to Christ, God has been gradually working on me, and thus my heart is in a different place today than the last time I read Paul's letters. Paul constantly confronts me about my excuses.

Oh, Our Excuses

There are few moments when Paul gives us direct glimpses into his view of helping the impoverished. This being the case, when he does, we should take a minute to contemplate what he is really saying, such as in the following passage:

But now I am traveling to Jerusalem, serving the saints. For Macedonia and Achaia were pleased to make some contribution for the poor among the saints in Jerusalem. For they were pleased to do so, and they are obligated to them. For if the Gentiles have shared in their spiritual things, they ought also to serve them in material things. Therefore, after I have accomplished this and sealed this fruit for delivery to them, I will depart by way of you for Spain.

(Romans 15:25–28)

For Paul, giving to the impoverished is a natural and necessary result of his ministry. There seems to be no option for him but traveling to Jerusalem to bring funds to the church, so that they may alleviate local poverty. We are *called* to contribute to the needs of others.

Paul is also pleased about giving—as we should be too. Giving is a satisfying opportunity, not a burden. Paul notes that the Christians in Macedonia and Achaia should be satisfied by the opportunity to help the impoverished in Jerusalem. Similarly, sharing in spiritual things should prompt us to share our belongings: Paul notes that the non-Jewish (Gentile) Christians in Macedonia and Achaia benefited from the initial efforts of the Jewish Christians in Jerusalem and, thus, should respond in kind. The sharing of physical belongings is a way for them to thank the church in Jerusalem for their efforts.

Paul the Fundraiser

In his letter to the Galatians, we see Paul again mention his fundraising efforts for the Jerusalem church. "[The apostles in Jerusalem] asked only that we should remember the poor, the very thing I was also eager to do" (Galatians 2:10).

Nestled in his letter to the Galatians—where he is discussing his dispute with Saint Peter—Paul tells us this seemingly random bit of information. It is here that we learn that giving to the impoverished was basically a given for Paul—as were his fundraising efforts to make it happen.

In his seemingly ad hoc detail in Galatians, there is a profound lesson: Giving to the impoverished shouldn't be something we have to argue ourselves into or convince other Christians of. Instead, it should be a given for all of us. Helping the impoverished should simply be part of what we do and how we live. If someone asks us if we care for the impoverished, we should be able to make a remark similar to Paul's—something like, "Of course, I am eager to help."

But if we're honest with ourselves, caring for the impoverished isn't a given for us. Often, we argue ourselves out of helping others. We convince ourselves that it's okay to let the problems of others stand—with a mere, "I'll pray for you"—when we could actually do so much more.

What Saint Paul Wants You to Get About Jesus and Poverty

> But just as you excel in everything—in faith and in speaking and in knowledge and with all diligence and in the love from us that is in you—so may you excel in this grace also. I am not saying this as a command, but proving the genuineness of your love by means of the diligence of others. For you know the grace of our Lord Jesus Christ, that although he was rich, for your sake he became poor, in order that you, by his poverty, may become rich.
>
> (2 Corinthians 8:7–9)

When Paul set out to explain to the Corinthians how they should handle difficult situations, help others, and share the good news of Jesus, he chose to center his message on grace. In making the case for living graciously, Paul pulls in the example of Jesus. He states that Jesus became poor for the sake of the world.

The first level of Jesus' poverty came in His decision to become a human. When Jesus decided to become human, He went from being crowned in glory to living amid humble circumstances on earth. He also went from being able to move as a spirit to being stuck in the limitations of the flesh. But Jesus took it on gladly, for our sakes. Additionally, Jesus became poor in a very ordinary way: He was born poor in Bethlehem, lived in poor Nazareth, and became a traveling preacher.

Jesus understood that it was by enduring poverty that He would be able to reach and save humanity. On His way to dying for the world—on the cross—Jesus became a poor man. Those of us who have much must realize how incredibly far we actually are from the state Jesus lived in. We must also keep in mind that our impoverished neighbors understand many things about Jesus that we do not.

This is not to say that to be poor is to be more holy in God's eyes. There are plenty of wealthy people who have done amazing things for the kingdom of God. It is about the state of the heart, *the willingness* to do whatever it takes for the gospel to spread.

If Paul were alive today, he would probably remind us of exactly the same thing he brought up to the Corinthians: Be gracious, for Jesus was incredibly gracious to us. Do what you can for those in need. Be kind to others, despite whatever dispute you have with them. Spread the good news of Jesus at all costs.

Giving Is a Three-Way Street—Between Us, Others, and God

We often think of giving as a one-way activity, but Paul sees it very differently. For Paul, the work of God is not a linear process but a cycle. When we give, it's not just the receivers who get a gift—we do also.

> The one who sows sparingly will also reap sparingly, and the one who sows bountifully will also reap bountifully. Each one should give as he has decided in his heart, not reluctantly or from compulsion, for God loves a cheerful giver. And God is able to cause all grace to abound to you, so that in everything at all times, because you have enough of everything, you may overflow in every good work. Just as it is written, "He scattered widely, he gave to the poor; his righteousness remains forever."
> (2 Corinthians 9:6–9; see Psalm 112:9)

If you give much, for the right reasons, you will receive much. Accordingly, you should give what you feel led to give. But Paul cautions us that God wants us to be cheerful givers.

God is abundantly gracious to givers; if you give what you feel led to give, you will have more than enough. For Paul, when we learn to give, we will overflow in every good work. Moreover, giving to others is an expression of righteousness.

When you summarize Paul's words in such simple terms, his statements suddenly become both shocking and hard to believe. ("Could God really view giving this way?" we may ask.) Giving is a fundamental law and order of God. It is how the world is meant to function. Nothing that we hold is truly ours; instead, what we have (everything we have) is a gift to steward—it should be shared. (Compare Luke 19:11–27.)

In continuing his statements about why the Corinthian church should give to the Jerusalem church, Paul says:

> Now the one who supplies seed to the sower and bread for food will provide and multiply your seed, and will cause the harvest of your righteousness to grow, being made rich in every way for all generosity, which is producing through us thanksgiving to God, because the service of this ministry is not only supplying the needs of the saints, but also is overflowing through many expressions of thanksgiving to God. Through the proven character of this service they will glorify God because of the submission of your confession to the gospel of Christ and the generosity of your participation toward them and toward everyone, and they are longing for you in their prayers for you, because of the surpassing grace of God to you. Thanks be to God for his indescribable gift!
>
> (2 Corinthians 9:10–15)

Paul doesn't put up with our insecurities about giving. Instead, he says that we should have confidence in God's ability to provide—and again indicates that when we give, God will multiply what we have. In addition, the effects of our giving will be multiplied by God.

Giving causes us and other people to overflow with thanksgiving to God. Others will be prompted to glorify God as a result of our generosity—it will remind them of our obedience to Jesus. Paul even goes so far as to indicate that giving to others causes them to pray for us—as does people's observance of God at work in us. Of course, it is not we who deserve any praise but God who gave us the resources in the first place. We are only able to give that which was already given to us. God is also the source of our salvation in Jesus—and thus our freedom not just to alleviate physical poverty but also to overcome spiritual poverty.

Paul confronts us with the reality that giving is itself an incredible gift. It prompts us to look to Jesus and glorify Him—to acknowledge His remarkable work among us, in both the spiritual and physical things. God is at work in all things. He is to be praised—for when we give to others, all sorts of possibilities are opened up. The cycle of poverty can be ended and the cycle of our lives can be transformed in the process.

Through Christ, each of us has the opportunity to initiate the alleviation of poverty in our communities and around the world—as Paul himself did. For some, this means a calling of full-time ministry. For others, this means living as a tentmaker—creating jobs through the ownership of a business and devoting the rest of our time to ministry and investing in others, as well as giving our money to poverty alleviation. And for still others, this means earning our income by working for someone else and using our time and resources to empower people. But for all of us, this means living as Jesus would have us to, in all things.

THE FIRST CHRISTIAN ENTREPRENEUR

If a man were to venture across the world starting businesses and communities, and his legacy lived beyond his life, we would consider him a tycoon. If that same man were to do these things for the betterment of others and risk his own life in the process, we would think of him as a daring social entrepreneur or a great humanitarian. And, if that man's primary motivation was to serve Jesus, we would consider him a godly entrepreneur.

There was such a godly entrepreneur who did all these things. His name was Paul, and he was a church planter.

Here are some of the habits that led to Paul's success. As people looking to overcome spiritual and physical poverty by truly loving others, we should live by the same habits—whether our calling is full-time ministry or not. (The activity of Paul's life went back and forth between ministry and business. At times, he devoted himself full-time to the preaching of the gospel, and at other times, he worked as a tentmaker to earn his living.)

No Job Is Too Lowly

Paul's entire ministry life was entrepreneurial. He had to raise capital, which, again, often meant doing the regular, lowly job of tent-making (see Acts 18:3)—and remember that he even went so far as to raise additional capital for others when needed (see, for example, Romans 15:25–27). Paul had to gain the respect of others (see, for example, Acts 9:26–31), and training people was a regular part of his routine (see 1 Timothy and Titus;

compare 1 Corinthians 1:10–17). Paul considered no job beneath him and no concern too small to deal with. (See, for example, 2 Corinthians 2:5–11.)

Do What You Can't Control

Right after Paul's conversion, he embraced the Holy Spirit's role in his life. (See Acts 9:19–22.) Unashamed of the Spirit's work—and boasting in what God had done for him (see, for example, Romans 5:1–5; 15:17–20; Philippians 2:14–18)—he went about the work of continuing Jesus' ministry. He openly told others to embrace spiritual gifts and the Spirit's leading, in full knowledge that no person can control God or what He will do in their lives. (See, for example, 1 Corinthians 12–13.)

For Paul, his vocation often meant pursuing ministry endeavors that he could not have anticipated—doing the completely unexpected, including traveling overseas. It also meant that his very work would often be completely unpredictable, very difficult, and something outside of his control.

Lean into Your Identity

Entrepreneurs are notoriously industrious and single-minded, and Paul was no different. His belief that eternal life started here, with acceptance of Jesus—meaning that nothing on this earth, including death, could make a serious dent in God's work—resulted in an unquenchable desire to do good for Jesus. (See Romans 6:1–23.) For example, even when a prophet tied himself up to symbolically represent Paul's future imprisonment in Jerusalem, Paul was not dissuaded from his mission of going to that city with the gospel. (See Acts 21:10–16.) There was no stopping this man. He knew from the beginning that he must suffer for Christ's sake (see Acts 9:16), and he fully embraced that calling, just as Christ Himself did His own mission.

Have Confidence in Your Role and Calling

Paul openly accepted his call as an apostle and never apologized for it. (See, for example, Romans 1:1.) This does not mean that he didn't explain his role or how it came to be—for he regularly did that (see, for example, Acts 26; Galatians 1:11–24)—but it does mean that Paul was confident in who he was before God and what God intended for him to do.

When it came time to say the difficult things or make the inevitably trying moves, Paul did so. (See, for example, Acts 15:36–41; Galatians 2:11–14.) He was confident that he could do so because he knew who Christ had made him to be and what Christ had asked of him. For Paul, there was no difference between his mission and God's mission—his identity was completely wrapped up in Christ's work.

Know Thyself

When it came to ministering to others, Paul was as open about his weaknesses as he was the role Christ had called him to. (See, for example, 2 Corinthians 12:1–10.) Paul regularly emphasized that his strength was found in Christ, not himself. (See, for example, Philippians 4:13.) Paul may have been confident, but he was also humble. Few can say that.

When it came time for Paul to defend Jesus, he did so by claiming all that Christ had done to transform him from a wretched hater into a loving saint. (See, for example, 1 Corinthians 15:1–11.) Paul knew who he was, on all counts. Prayer and self-reflection—or, better put, reflecting on Christ and comparing himself to Him—showed Paul regularly what must be done next and where he stood in his faith journey.

Sacrifice

Great leaders are never afraid to give of themselves first. They know they must lead by example. Paul was this type of leader. When difficult work had to be done, Paul fully embraced that part of his calling too—even when the work included proclaiming the gospel under threatening circumstances and being falsely arrested and beaten by authorities who misunderstood his motives. (See, for example, Acts 22.) When it came to something as trying as wrongful imprisonment for being a Christian, Paul took on the task. Not only did he embrace his role as a sufferer for Christ, but he also made the most of it—ministering to those also imprisoned, to guards, and to others through his writings. (See, for example, Acts 16:16–34; 2 Timothy 1:8–18.) Much of what we have today from Paul was written while he was in prison. He led by example, even when it was painful to do so. He could do this because Jesus was his example.

I've Met People like Paul

There is a group of pastors in Bihar, India, who are living Paul's values. These pastors are facing a great challenge: there are millions of people in Bihar who have never even heard the name of Jesus. I have met over a dozen pastors there—and they have changed my life. Each time, it was like meeting Paul, Sosthenes, Timothy, or Titus.

One pastor said, "I lead six churches in five villages and three small groups. I also oversee five Bible studies, water well programs, an empowering women program (where they're learning to be tailors and seamstresses), and a literacy training program for children; and we're starting a literacy training program for adults." I was flabbergasted.

Another said, "We're reaching out to villages who have never heard the name of Jesus," and "The message is empowering people—they're being healed and finding a new life."

"I was very sick—nearly dead," explained yet another pastor. "Then he [pointing to a leader of Transformation India Movement] came and prayed for me, and now I am well. Today, I am back to preaching each day. I am proclaiming the good news of what Jesus has done for me and can do for them."

"There are women who are finding hope again for themselves and their children in the gospel of Jesus," expressed one more pastor. "They're seeing that Jesus can change their lives for the better and embracing the gospel."

The good news of Jesus is transforming lives. Stories like these are just a few of hundreds. But these stories don't just motivate me; they convict me.

Hearing about the work of these church planters in Bihar has made me admit to myself that I am not as hardworking for the kingdom of God as I thought I was, and furthermore that I actually know very little about the kingdom. I don't say this to be self-depreciating—in some kind of false humility; I actually mean it. Meeting church planters in Bihar is like meeting people who live like Paul, Barnabas, and Timothy. It has made me realize, as we all should, that no matter what our calling is, we have a long way to go. And that Jesus wants to work on our hearts to get us where we need to be. No matter what our specific calling, He will use it for His glory, but we must first be willing to admit our weaknesses and be used by Him.

Thus, regardless of what your precise calling is, Christ wants all of you—He wants to capture your every thought. (See 2 Corinthians 10:5.) He wants to overcome spiritual and physical poverty in you and in the lives of others. He wants to change the world through your life. Whatever trouble you encounter in the process, He can overcome it.

REFLECTIONS ON PART TWO: JESUS WANTS TO CHANGE THE WORLD THROUGH YOU

When faced with the big problems of poverty, it's easy to believe that there is little that can be done. It can all feel so overwhelming. But there are solutions. The answer comes back to you and to me: what are *we* going to do?

The biblical view of poverty is that everything starts with relationship. And out of those relationships, churches and businesses can grow. They can change the spiritual and physical economy of an entire community.

The biblical view of poverty is that the sacrifices we make *can* change the life of another. Jesus is asking me, and He is asking you, "What are you willing to give? Are you willing to give to the point that it hurts?"

The biblical view is that we should be smart in our giving. We should aim to empower other people. We should consider how God can use the workplace for great good. We should consider the power of living bi-vocationally as missionaries for Jesus, each and every day. We should think of Jesus' work not as something we will do someday, but something we can do every day—in how we give, shop, and act.

Jesus' economy is based on self-sacrifice. His currency is love.

By creating jobs, planting churches, and meeting basic needs, we can renew communities with Jesus' love. We can, in a real and tangible way, join Jesus in creating an economy that reflects His values.

But to do Jesus' work, we need to combat the myths of poverty with truth.

PART THREE

The myths of poverty.
What followers of Jesus should say in response.
And *really* understanding poverty.

THE MYTHS OF POVERTY

The men who had the night shift at our local homeless shelter were dragging the green mats out onto the linoleum floor for people to sleep on. I tried to not let the scratching sound and movement all around me distract me from my prayer. In front of me was Pedro, age fifty or so, who had the weather-battered face of a man who had lived through too many winters on the street and too many summers in the fields. His pay was never enough to last the winter. Pedro suddenly blurted out, "I just wonder if God chose this fate for me." Then he looked up and shouted, "God, did You do this to me?" The men dragging the green mats stopped for a moment, looked at me, and then continued their task. I knew half of them were homeless, too, and were probably thinking the same thing.

"God, did You do this to me?" It was one of the most honest expressions to God I have ever heard. Pedro had voiced the superstitious fear that often lurks in the back of many of our minds: "God, did You ruin my life?" I thought to myself, "Who is to blame for this man's poverty?"

We all have biases and false views of God. We all have misunderstandings about what God wants to accomplish in our lives. This is true no matter what our income level is or how spiritually mature we are.

Because the reality of poverty in our own lives is so hard to reconcile, we often attempt to make sense of it by generating falsehoods regarding God, our situation, and our spiritual health. Here are nine examples of the myths we create and the biblical answers to them.

I. "God Chose This Destiny for Me"

Despite how it may seem, God doesn't choose poverty for anyone—it is a result of the fallen world we live in. (See Genesis 3.) God doesn't want poverty for us; He desires for all people to live full lives. We know this to be the case because the ultimate fulfillment of the good news of Jesus is seen in a new heaven and new earth, where all pain—and lack of intimacy with God—are removed:

> And I saw a new heaven and a new earth, for the first heaven and the first earth had passed away, and the sea did not exist any longer. And I saw the holy city, new Jerusalem, coming down out of heaven from God, prepared like a bride adorned for her husband. And I heard a loud voice from the throne saying, "Behold, the dwelling of God is with humanity, and he will take up residence with them, and they will be his people and God himself will be with them. And he will wipe away every tear from their eyes, and death will not exist any longer, and mourning or wailing or pain will not exist any longer. The former things have passed away."
>
> (Revelation 21:1–4)

It is God's plan to remove every tear from our world. In this context, poverty is too severe and sad of a problem to be ignored. Although God didn't choose poverty for the world, He embraced the impoverished, as one of the impoverished, in order to heal humanity. Christ has overcome the world and will ultimately make all things right. It is our job to proclaim this in our actions.

2. "My Problems Are Merely Physical"

Every struggle we have has some underlying spiritual element. The struggles of this world are representative of both our need for a savior (Jesus) and our longing for His return, when He will bring about the end of death and sin and restore peace to our world. Physical poverty is not special in this regard. It is just one of many things affected by spiritual issues. For example, addiction can have physical causes and symptoms, but it is also a spiritual problem. Underneath addiction is almost always some sort of past trauma, something that created an ongoing emotional burden. Addictions are often attempts to alleviate this type of pain. And how did that pain begin? Usually, it started with a sinful person, troubled by spiritual matters, inflicting pain on another person.

Likewise, physical poverty can be caused by sin in (or surrounding) a person's life—damaging relationships and unhealthy financial dependencies come to mind as examples—but is also caused by the larger problem of sin in our world. Since the beginning of humanity, people of every generation have failed to look out for each other or consider others' needs before their own. We have misused resources for personal gain, often at the expense of the vulnerable. These are spiritual problems at their core; they reflect our spiritual poverty.

That is why, when God works in our lives on a spiritual plane, our physical problems can improve in the process. When we come to understand our identity in Christ, as belonging to His kingdom, we learn to cast aside our self-focused behavior. The impact of this process is exponential in our lives and in the lives we affect.

Many of the issues associated with problems in the physical world are rooted in our misunderstandings of Jesus and what He wants to do among us. When we address the spiritual issues, we can begin to see things from God's perspective and start to make wiser decisions; Jesus can heal us and set us free from the captivity of sin. (See, for example, Luke 4:18–19.) Granted, disease and pain will still exist—because we live in a fallen world (which fell due to humanity's choices to oppose God). But by letting God handle our spiritual problems, we will see more clearly the root of the physical problems in our lives and the lives of others.

It is unfair to say that a singular instance of physical poverty is indicative of unaddressed sin in a person's life. Yet the broad-stroke effect of humanity's distance from God and His plan has undoubtedly caused much of the poverty we see today. The pages of the Bible, as well as those of our history books (if the same logic is applied), are ripe with evidence of devastation caused by humanity's selfishness and desire for independence from God. Whether we are the victims or the perpetrators of this devastation, the root cause remains the same. The farther we stray from God, the more dire the results. After all, "the wages of sin is death, but the free gift of God is eternal life in Christ Jesus our Lord" (Romans 6:23 ESV). This free gift is something we must grab hold of if we are to truly conquer poverty in our world.

3. "God Chose for Me to be Sick—And I Always Will Be"

The reality of sickness is that it generally comes from one of three places: an absence of support from others to alleviate our illnesses, the choices we make (such as choosing to eat poorly or follow unsafe practices), or the fallen state of our world (and the environment we live in).

For those living in the first category, faulty logistics, inadequate resources, or a lack of compassion have kept people from coming alongside them. The truth of the matter is that all of us with wealth and/or physical ability have the opportunity to work with those in physical poverty to bring sanitation, water, bed nets, medical clinics, healthy living training, and so forth. These things alone will prevent many (if not most) of the illnesses in the developing world. We have the opportunity to come alongside the suffering in the developed world as well. The sick and the impoverished are struggling in our communities too. I have heard shocking stories of people in the late stages of illness coming home alone to empty houses full of dirty dishes and piles of laundry. I have seen the elderly stuck in homes with no transportation to buy groceries or get their medication. No one was able or willing to help them. This is where we can be a voice for the marginalized. We can come alongside these people as the hands and feet of Jesus in our world.

For those who are sick because of the choices they have made, showing them unselfish (and giving) love will help them rise out of poverty. Likewise, programs that holistically deal with a person's poverty—both their spiritual and physical poverty—and alleviate it through the power of Jesus can change the way they currently live and help them make better choices for the future.

As far as our fallen world is concerned, due to humanity's choices, the reality is that some sickness will always exist—just as some poverty will always exist—but that shouldn't discourage us from doing something about it. Ultimately, it will be our Lord who overcomes all physical and spiritual poverty, and our work with Him is a type of firstfruits in this process.

4. "My Sin Brought Me Here"

Sin can certainly result in poverty issues—and yes, sin is the reason why poverty exists in general, because it was introduced into the world when humanity rebelled against God. But if sin directly resulted in poverty, many of the richest people in the world would be poor.

Many people live in generational poverty, where their family has, for years, lived off of government checks; or their family has, for years, believed that what they have is all that they will ever have. Both of these situations are also a type of societal poverty. Society tells people their value by dictating their place in the world, and thus people stay where they are. This is especially an issue in societies where religions dictate the value of certain lives. But this is also the case when government checks make it too easy for people to keep living in poverty—or even incentivize laziness.

The reality is that we are created to work and to be free—any system that impedes people from doing so is inherently flawed and likely the workings of evil in "compassionate" clothing.

We must combat the idea that a person's individual sinning, alone, is what creates their poverty. Instead, it's a sinful world—and a sinful humanity. If it takes a village to raise a child, it usually takes a society (making evil choices) to create an impoverished person.

5. "The Wealthier Are More Loved than I Am—and Perhaps Smarter"

Jesus lived as a poor man and ministered to the impoverished, and God often talks about bringing justice for the poor. Thus, it's clear that Jesus believes in the impoverished and loves them deeply.

There is no biblical evidence that wealth is a sign of God's love. At times, it is a sign of His blessing—but that doesn't mean He has some sadistic game going where He chooses wealth for some but not for others. Our world is much more complex than that.

In reality, where wealth exists and where it doesn't is related to a host of issues, from geography, to weather, to insects, to governmental issues, to trade agreements, to warfare (or lack thereof). The wealthier aren't naturally smarter than the impoverished and the wealthier are not more loved by God. In fact, wealth acquired through dishonest gain is detested by God. (See, for example, Proverbs 13:11; 20:21, 23.)

There is enough wealth in the world to overcome physical poverty. There just isn't enough motivation. If your heart isn't in the right place, it's hard to convince yourself to do something for someone who can give you little or nothing in return. That's why Paul says this:

> For only rarely will someone die on behalf of a righteous person (for on behalf of a good person possibly someone might even dare to die), but God demonstrates his own love for us, in that while we were still sinners, Christ died for us.   (Romans 5:7–8)

The wealthy, including me, must realize that no matter how they became wealthy, they have an obligation to the impoverished. They have a gift or opportunity and should use it for good.

6. "I Am Worth Less than Others" (or "My Community Is Worth Less than Other Communities")

There couldn't be anything further from the truth than the lie that one person, or one community, is worth less to God—or the world— than others. Jesus came for all of us, every single one of us. Despite what oppressors in our world may say or what any one person may claim, Jesus views all people as equal. Paul emphasizes this point:

> There is neither Jew nor Greek, there is neither slave nor free, there is neither male and female, for you are all one in Christ Jesus. And if you are Christ's, then you are descendants of Abraham, heirs according to the promise.   (Galatians 3:28–29)

We are all equal under God. And we must combat any ideas, people, or systems that say otherwise. Inequality is not just a dangerous idea—it is an evil one.

7. "I Can't Do Anything About the Corruption in My Society"

One of the steps to alleviating poverty is to combat the myth that corruption is something we can't put an end to. Corruption alleviation starts with each of us living ethically and mentoring others to do the same. (It's incredible how many positive changes this can bring.) It continues with diplomacy, the quick and important work of justice, and the showing of mercy through incredible acts of sustainable compassion. However, it is ultimately Christ who transforms lives completely—and thus our work to alleviate corruption must incorporate the gospel.

We should never allow corruption to hold us back from taking action. Instead, we must act to set a better example—a life lived the way Jesus would have us to live.

8. "No One Cares About My Struggles"

One of the lies we tell ourselves is that no one cares about our problems. As suicide rates climb higher and higher in the Unites States,[6] I can't help but see a correlation between the lie that "no one cares" and self-destructive behavior.

I have heard both the physically and spiritually impoverished tell me that no one cares about them. We absolutely must work to combat this idea, because low self-esteem can lead to all kinds of evil and can allow for evil to continue unchecked.

If you really break down the things that have led to sins in your life, I am betting that you can track them all back to a lie that someone told you or you told yourself. And it probably went something like this: "I'm alone," "No one cares about me," or "No one is here to help me."

Most of us are held back from realizing our dreams by a faulty view of ourselves. We don't recognize or acknowledge the way God sees us, and, as a result, we settle for less than we're meant to be. In fact, sometimes we turn into the very thing we feared we would become.

---

6. Centers for Disease Control and Prevention (CDC), "Suicide Rising Across the US," CDC *Vitalsigns*, June 2018, https://www.cdc.gov/vitalsigns/pdf/vs-0618-suicide-H.pdf (accessed September 22, 2018).

Jesus cares about us. He loves us and wants to walk with us. He wants to reverse the cycles of spiritual and physical poverty we find ourselves in every day. It is the Holy Spirit who does this work in our lives. And those of us seeking to alleviate poverty should follow the Spirit's example and be willing to walk with people out of poverty—acknowledging our own poverty in the process and noting how the Spirit is overcoming it in us.

9. "No Matter How Good My Ideas Are, They Will Never Go Anywhere"

One of the saddest things to witness is someone who is defeated. In my experience, most people who feel defeated believe that their ideas aren't any good and that they will never go anywhere. I think people believe this only because no one has walked with them in the process of overcoming opposition. Consequently, they remain bound by the fears and self-doubt that are so prevalent in our world.

There are answers to all of the questions and doubts of our hearts. Jesus offers us a new identity, free of these burdens. Likewise, there are answers to every single one of the problems of poverty. These answers are found by loving people like Jesus does and telling people how much He loves them. We must provide an alternative to the worldviews that result in poverty—that alternative is Christ and charitable living.

God wants good for your life. He wants to offer you eternal life that starts now. Deny the hopelessness in favor of hope. Affirm Christ reigning in all of areas of your life and see where it takes you. And then pass the gift along; give that hope to someone else.

Put simply, we end poverty by first affirming God's belief in us and then taking action to create the economy Jesus envisions.

THE CHURCH AT THE CENTER OF SOLVING POVERTY

Throughout the world, corruption is a problem that perpetually destroys progress. This is especially true in developing-world communities, which are already vulnerable to exploitation due to their marginal economic position.

Those living in poverty desperately need assistance in alleviating corruption. This assistance could very well come through existing local churches. But since these churches are very poor themselves, outside funding in the form of grants is needed. Here are five ways that healthy churches can make life better for those living in developing-world communities. This is a vision for healthy Christian communities (that's my definition of "churches") in impoverished places.

1. Ethics for a Whole Community

Jesus calls Christians to a high standard of ethical living. The ethics of Christianity are intended to be applied to all situations with all people—loving your neighbor and, thus, treating them as Jesus would treat them. This baseline view of others can create an ethical foundation for a community that originates from a healthy church.

2. Training and Education for the Community

Strong Christian communities are safe havens for training and learning. Healthy church communities create trust-based environments, ideal for education. Christian teachers see discipleship as part of Jesus' mode; thus, training others becomes second nature to those with the spiritual gifts of teaching and discipleship. These two factors, combined, make churches an ideal hub for training and education for an entire community.

Imagine if church planters were to receive leadership training. They could then train entrepreneurs in biblical ethics—and, by extension, teach business leaders how to take the best care of their employees. Add fair trade standards, regular reporting, and accountability to the mix, and you have a winning scenario.

3. Aid and Relief, Properly Offered and Regulated

Aid and general poverty relief often happen through the church. Traditionally, churches have always been on the front lines of the fight against poverty. Churches are full of people ready to volunteer their time for the betterment of the lives of others.

Knowing that churches are actively involved in this work can make things a lot easier for a foreigner who wants to bring aid to a community. They need only ask the local congregation what is already being done and what they can help with. Our goal, as outsiders coming into a community, should always be to empower what local leaders are doing or help facilitate a dream of theirs that they can take ownership of and lead.

4. The Revealing, and Meeting, of Real Needs

Real needs are often revealed, and known, through local church leaders. They are the eyes and ears of the community, right in the middle of everything that's going on. The church is like a layer cake; you should be able to take out a slice and see *all* the layers of a community—all the ages, all the ethnicities, all the occupations—gathered together in one body. Healthy churches really get to know, and love, their communities. They are a source of advice and healing for the problems that occur. In the process of fulfilling this role, they become valuable resources for understanding their communities' true needs. In a situation foreign to the developed-world investor, this knowledge is vital to success. A church can point them to the greatest needs and the safest places to invest (those without corruption).

5. Accountability and Transparency for Economic Development

Accountability and transparency are core principles of Christian living; through the church, these principles can be extended to others in a community. Christians can serve as a hub for bringing accountability to the lives of others. They can serve as those who ask for transparency, first from the people in their congregations and then from everyone they work with. (In the model of the nonprofit Jesus' Economy, we simultaneously work with entrepreneurs and church planters in the same community. Christian church leaders serve as accountability partners and ethical trainers for the entrepreneurs we support, to ensure that the standards of Jesus' Economy are upheld.)

The church can make a massive difference in our efforts to alleviate poverty. By embracing not just Christian principles but also the Christian community as the place to overcome spiritual and physical poverty, we can make our world a better place. It is my belief that as we create jobs or meet basic needs, the church must stand in the center of our efforts. Otherwise, our efforts will not be sustainable. We must disciple others as Jesus has called us to do.

REFLECTIONS ON PART THREE: WHERE THE PHYSICAL AND SPIRITUAL MEET

The spiritual and physical are interconnected. Spiritual poverty is always, in some way, at work behind physical poverty. Our world is spiritually deprived of the full love of God. If humanity were in true relationship with God, there would be no poverty.

That is God's end goal: the end of tears, the end of mourning, and the end of poverty.

This is the trajectory of the Bible—that Jesus' economy, His kingdom, is breaking into our world and one day will fully come to be.

Jesus has an entirely different economy in mind. Every time we substitute the narrative of poverty with God's story, a little more of His economy comes into the world. Each time we offer Jesus' currency of love, His economy becomes a reality—in that very place, at that very time. We see a little glimpse of God's kingdom in each mouth fed, in each drop of clean water provided, in each woman empowered, in each ethical business created, in each family given the ability to help themselves.

This is the business of the church: to bring Jesus' economy to this world. The church should be the center of alleviating poverty. When the Christian sees scarcity, he or she should see that as an opportunity to bring the love of Jesus. The Christian should see opportunity when others see despair. The Christian should see assets in a community when all others see only turmoil.

When you face the idea of scarcity in your own life, remember this: scarcity will one day lose, and abundance—life itself—will win.

Jesus doesn't look at the world from the perspective of scarcity, but instead from the view of abundance. Following His example, we ask the following: "What assets are here?" "How can we use them for good?" "How can we show love by using everything at our disposal for Jesus?" "How can we live Jesus' economy?" "How can we bring Jesus' economy to this place?" These are the types of questions we ask ourselves and whose answers we try to live out, through confidence in Jesus' power to make these visions a reality.

With our simple, everyday choices, we can make the world a better place. We can live Jesus' currency of love.

PART FOUR

Some *very* practical ideas for overcoming poverty.
How you can truly love people.
And why it won't be easy.

TRULY LOVING YOUR NEIGHBORS AND NEIGHBORHOOD

I want to see everyone get involved in effectively alleviating poverty in their local community. But when you're considering getting involved, think about your motivations. Know your weaknesses and your limits, as well as your strengths. If you don't come to terms with yourself, you might get into a situation where you're actually causing someone more harm than good.

Discerning Gifts

Have you discerned your gifts within your local Christian community? (See, for example, 1 Corinthians 12–14; Ephesians 4:7–16.) Do you know what your specific calling in the church is? If not, you really should spend some time thinking about these things, asking your pastor and local elders to pray over you and to work with you. It is difficult to know how God wants to use you if you don't understand how God created you.

But don't use the discernment process as an excuse not to get involved—or to not listen to the Spirit in the moment. Discernment happens both through prayer and action—I want to encourage you to do both these things, and to be cautious, ensuring that you truly learn how God created you and the gifts He has given you. I'm suggesting that you contemplate, pray, and discern the precise way God made you—this will make you much more effective for His kingdom.

Also, it's worth noting that only you and God really know what you are gifted at, and this can be discerned only in community and in prayer. As much as we should seek and rely on the advice of pastors and mentors (who are humans and can sometimes be wrong), we must ultimately trust the path that God has revealed in our hearts. We cannot wait for the validation of others to act on what we know to be true, through prayer and discernment. If we are genuinely desiring to serve Him, not ourselves, He will lead us down a path of righteousness—and those who know Him will be able to recognize His leading in our lives. Thus, I'm advocating for balance: discernment through individual prayer (you alone with God) *and* through group prayer and discussion. God speaks both to us individually and through his church collectively.

Start with Loving Your Neighbor—And Really Meaning It

The best place to start a ministry—especially one geared toward poverty alleviation—is with the people you see every day: your physical neighbors. If your neighbors don't know you're a Christian, that's a problem. You don't have to parade your faith in front of people, but your neighbors should know that you are a resource for questions they have about faith in Jesus. They should be able to see you living your faith in action every day. You should be a light in the darkness that surrounds most people's daily lives—a Christ-centered refuge in the middle of the chaos.

Ask yourself these questions: "What are my neighbors' needs at the moment?" "How can I put in a good word for Jesus with them?" "What's difficult for them today?" "How can I empower them to overcome that difficulty?" "How can I walk alongside my neighbor in their pain and turmoil?" "How can I show them the face of Jesus through my example?"

It is incredible to me that once I started practicing loving my neighbors—which I learned from watching my wife love our neighbors—I suddenly understood how to better help others overcome physical and spiritual poverty.

In the process of searching for spiritual poverty in my neighborhood, I spotted the spiritual poverty in my own life. I realized that I am in no way superior to the people I am trying to love for Jesus—either my neighbors, the homeless, or the impoverished around the world.

Additionally, even while trying to help people in my neighborhood, I sometimes failed to truly empower them. This is perhaps best illustrated by a simple story.

My neighbor came over all flustered, telling me that her lawnmower was broken. Of course, I volunteered my lawn mower, which I lovingly called the Terminator because it had pieces of sheet metal and car license plates holding it together. But then I realized that she likely wouldn't be able to start it because the mower is so old and terrible.

To fix my blunder, I volunteered to run the mower myself. What I should have noticed is that my quick action caused her to feel anxious; she didn't appreciate the invasion of privacy, as I could have easily looked into her windows while mowing her lawn. It also made her feel embarrassed, since her backyard was quite overgrown at that point. Furthermore, my response was demeaning; she felt I was assuming she couldn't do it herself.

My dumb decision made my neighbor uncomfortable—made our relationship awkward for a while—and then ultimately forced her to buy a lawnmower right away, which she might not have been able to afford at that point. The simplest solution would have been to simply start the mower for her or show her son how to do so. Instead, I crossed the very clear line of doing something for someone that they could easily have done for themselves.

If you are ready to get involved with empowering the impoverished locally, consider how Jesus would alleviate poverty—in each and every decision. More often than not, the right way to love your neighbor is to begin with a conversation. Ask them what they're going through. Be sensitive to their feelings or their need for privacy but be willing to listen if they want to share. This is often more effective than anything you can actually do. It communicates your love for them. Most people don't need someone to solve their problems or tell them what they should be doing. Instead, they need someone to magnify the voice of God in their lives—to encourage them to listen to His guidance.

TRULY LOVING THE HOMELESS

It's never easy to approach poverty in a way that is truly empowering. Deciding that you're going to move beyond giving handouts makes things more difficult—but it's worth it if it means actually helping people. Here are some of the situations you will encounter and how I recommend you handle them.

I Meet a Homeless Person Who Needs Help—What Do I Do?

"John, there's this guy outside the parking garage every morning, slumped over, who looks kind of sickly. I'm pretty sure he's homeless. Today, I made him a sandwich and brought it to him. I'm not sure what else to do for him. You work with the homeless, right? What would you do?"

I am still making my morning coffee when a colleague asks me this question. This is the moment when I usually smile first. I'm about to tell her she shouldn't have given him the sandwich, but I don't want to crush whatever zeal is in her or make her feel guilty. I also don't want to look like the jerk who hates the homeless, because nothing could be further from the truth. In addition, I'm hoping that the lack of caffeine in me won't make my words harsher than I intend them to sound.

"For years, I gave people sandwiches," I begin, "until I realized that it made me feel good, but didn't make them better." She gulps a little too hard on her tea—I can tell it was too hot to swallow that fast. "Now, I tell them about the mission."

"The mission?" she says. "Yes, the mission," I reply. I'm a little surprised that she doesn't know about it—it's just a little ways down the street, albeit in a district you wouldn't walk in alone, especially in the evenings after work.

I ask her if she has ever considered getting a tour of our local rescue mission (homeless shelter). I tell her that nearly every mission in the country will give you a tour, if you just call and ask. And that it's safe to get one—they will escort you with people who know what they're doing. Often, the executive director will offer the tour.

"But I want to help," she replies. I tell her that the best way for her to help is to become informed, give financially to the mission (if she believes in it, after the tour), consider volunteering there ("They almost always need volunteers," I say), and to then spread the word to the homeless people she meets.

I also ask that she be careful what time of day she has conversations with homeless people who seem unstable, advise that she wait to do so when others are with her, and urge that she never engage in conversations in isolated areas where people cannot see the conversation going on.

She mentions that she has encountered several homeless people in the alley behind our building, when going out the back door. I tell her that I, too, have seen and talked with them. I then say that in that particular instance, it is best for her to simply keep walking, while saying hello, making eye contact, and being cordial of course. She is a bit surprised that I don't encourage her to engage in conversation in this instance.

I Would Say the Same to You, and More

Under similar circumstances, I would give you the same advice I gave my colleague. But if we had more time to talk than a short, coffee-machine conversation, I would tell you a few other things too:

To start, you're no help to anyone if you get hurt helping people. It will probably keep you from ever reaching out again and scare away others from reaching out too—so don't think you're invincible. I have often heard people use the excuse that God will protect them. While God will ultimately look out for you, He gave us common sense for a reason.

Be aware of your surroundings, be evaluative, and be vigilant. I am not implying that all homeless people are dangerous. Far from it. However, those who continually choose to live on the street, even though programs are available to them, are sometimes doing so because of severe addictions or mental instability. In a bad moment, or when feeling threatened, unstable people can become dangerous. Sometimes you won't even know what triggered a person to become hostile. It could be that you remind them of someone they know or that they are threatened by your body language. My point is that you should take caution: make sure that you're safe and that you do what you can in your power to make the other person know you are a safe person for them to have a conversation with.

That said, there is not really anything to be afraid of if you engage in conversation in the right context and place—preferably where other people are around. Just be aware of your surroundings and your body language, and never make someone feel cornered. Additionally, please don't use fear as an excuse for not listening to the Holy Spirit. I have been in lots of dangerous situations for the sake of Jesus, because the Spirit asked me to—but I always do everything I can to make those dangerous situations as safe as they can be.

When helping the homeless, it is critical to understand the psychology of the population you're talking to, as well as their social norms. It is also important to be prepared to provide them with good answers to their questions.

What You Want to Know, Learn from Your Local Mission (Homeless Shelter)

When you visit your local mission, here's what you want to find out: Ask how they address the issues homeless people often have in their lives— like addiction or broken relationships. Ask if they offer resources such as counseling, job-skill training, or some sort of discipleship program. If your homeless mission doesn't offer any of these services, ask them who does. Remember this information, and even put the contact numbers for local services in your phone, so that the next time you meet a homeless person, you will know where and who to direct them to. You will be surprised how many homeless people don't know about the resources at their disposal—you can be everything to them by spreading knowledge.

The Psychology of Perpetual Homelessness

Despite all of the local resources that may be at the disposal of homeless people, this won't change the fact that you may hear excuses about why they won't take advantage of particular services. Be ready for this and explain to them that you simply don't give out cash—instead, note to them that you support these services because those who provide them are the true experts at empowering people. You can also note for homeless people you meet that they should try checking out the services again, because they never know when things may have changed for the better.

When you really look at people instead of the sign they are holding, you begin to truly *see* the person. When you make eye contact with someone, you treat them as a human being. You give them dignity.

After some time interacting with people, you will begin to be able to distinguish between the people who genuinely want help and the people who don't. Because, it's true that some people simply want money; they don't really care about getting off the street. The mistake, though, is to assume that is the case for the majority of people, because it's not.

I come from a rather small town with a bleeding heart. We are located in a pass-through area with a lot of transient people on their way to somewhere else. Our town seems to have more nonprofits per capita than any town in the U.S., and that makes transient homeless people stick around. But because we're a smaller town, faces don't blend into the crowd as easily as in big cities.

For example, I've seen a "homeless" woman who's been pregnant, according to her sign, on and off for five years. Yet she never has any children around her, and I've seen her going off several times to a stash in the woods. She was also "out of gas" by the local grocery store for two years before her pregnancies. I'm sure I don't need to explain this racket to you.

I've had other homeless people tell me they won't go to the local rescue mission because of one reason or another. Afterward, I've asked the mission employees about that person and learned that they got kicked out because they wouldn't give up alcohol or drugs.

I've walked in the woods and seen camps completely covered in trash—having the most unsanitary conditions you can think of, with people disrespecting the land and themselves. So, yes, the racketeers are there. And that's why giving money to someone you don't know is almost always a terrible idea.

On the other hand, I've met people who've experienced a life tragedy like bankruptcy or a sudden family death that pushed them over the edge. I've met women fleeing from abusive spouses and immigrants trying to find a fresh start. These people needed help to overcome hurdles in their life on the way to becoming independent and contributing to society again. As we know, our current systems don't make it easy for people to become independent—especially if they are facing additional barriers, such as English as their non-native language, no family support system, depression or mental illness, substance-abuse withdrawal, unmet childcare needs, lack of transportation, and others. Hiring biases, unregulated rent pricing, and a lack of public transportation infrastructure can make coming out of poverty nearly impossible without additional financial aid.

When you see the faces of those living in poverty, my hope is that you will think of this latter group of people first: the people who really need and want to be empowered. But no matter whom you meet, the racketeer or the person in need, each one is a human being and deserves to be treated with dignity and respect. Conversation goes a longer way than a dollar bill, so start there.

Things You Should Know

Nearly every American city has some sort of support structure for the homeless. Many small towns do not, so the nearest city is your best outlet for helping a homeless person. Thus, if you're in a small town, paying for a homeless person's bus ticket so they can travel to a city and gain access to those resources can actually be a good idea. And if you pay for the bus ticket, then actually buy it—don't hand out cash.

Whether you're in a small town or a city, know the resources in your area. Besides visiting your local mission and asking questions, here's the easiest solution for learning the information that can help you truly love someone: ask a social worker. Talk to them and find out what resources are available in your town. This is the best way to begin to gain a holistic picture of what goes on in your community. However, if you don't know a social worker (or know someone who knows one), it's time to go to Google. Seriously, just start searching for "your town name + poverty" or "your town name + homeless" or "your town name + free medical." Your state's department of social or human services and the United Way are places to start as well. They usually provide printouts of services in local areas. I recommend carrying with you a list of their services with phone numbers and addresses (along with information on your local mission or shelter), so that you'll be ready with an answer for those in need.

For example, in my town, a person can get a free hot meal three times a day, every day. Young mothers can get counseling services, free or reduced-cost diapers, clothing, and formula. Domestic abuse victims can get counseling and support services. We have food cards and several food banks. There are discounted clothing stores and free back-to-work clothing boutiques. During the holidays, there are discounted toy shops, toy giveaways, and adopt-a-family trees. Kids with learning disorders or impediments can get free or reduced therapy. There's outreach for suicide prevention and services for at-risk teens. There's free financial aid training and budget coaching, and much, much more. I'm guessing you'll find that similar programs exist in your town if you look around for them.

You can also talk to your pastor. Your pastor is (hopefully!) informed about the nonprofits in your area—and the social services available—and can give you some basic information. Then, read the nonprofit websites and, if you have time, go take some tours. Nonprofits love to give tours—remember, they're always looking for donors—so you will have no problem learning about what they do.

But the best resource in your city—if there is one in your city—is always a mission. They're often called "Union Gospel Mission" or "Rescue Mission." It is going to be this group of people that combines a love of Jesus with assisting those in poverty.

A Different Cultural Reality

When I first started serving the homeless regularly—as a minister in a chapel at a rescue mission—I didn't understand homeless culture. I didn't even know there was a homeless culture. A very gruff-looking night-shift supervisor explained it to me, after I made several terrible blunders, including asking too many questions and asking people to tell me their life stories (how they became homeless).

Stereotypes, as we all know, fall short. Describing cultural norms has similar disadvantages: the describer is always biased and interpreting from their own perspective. Also, to even talk about a "norm," there are a certain number of assumptions that have to be made. That said, here are some thoughts on culture surrounding homelessness.

Understand that some homeless people you meet may not want to give their names. This could be because of a lack of trust of authorities of any kind, because they have done something in the past that is illegal, or because they are an illegal immigrant. But none of these things should stop us from showing love to people—do you really need to know someone's name to love them? Just because someone doesn't trust you enough to give you their real name doesn't mean that they won't listen to your advice.

Homeless people are often paranoid, and for very good reasons. They have usually had many bad things done to them. But they're also very tough. They have gone through so much that their endurance is admirable. Many homeless people also know an incredible amount about the Bible, theology, spirituality, and religion. They have seen evil firsthand, and they regularly respond to it by searching for reasons why it occurred. You will be shocked to learn that most homeless people will know more about your Bible than you will. I have an M.A. in Biblical Studies and yet have been schooled in Bible trivia by homeless guys. To survive on the street, you either have to be a little crazy or very smart—and sometimes both—so be ready to be schooled. Do not consider yourself smarter, because you're likely not.

In addition, in the U.S., there is sadly a large population of homeless veterans. They're dealing with any number of issues, from post-traumatic stress syndrome to the aftereffects of having been exposed to toxic substances. We have to be understanding of this. Most veterans will tell you that they are veterans. And whether or not they are willing to talk about their experience will often indicate how they feel about it. These are extremely complex issues—psychologically, for the veteran, and politically. The most important thing is to show them respect and thank them for their service. This will often lead to some level of trust on their part, which will allow you to have the opportunity to show them love.

Establishing respect and trust is critical for dealing with any population group, but especially among the homeless.

Be Meek, Not Weak

"Sit down!" I yelled to the homeless guy in the back. He was screaming at me because he disagreed with what I was preaching. He quietly sat back down, with a thump, in the plastic chair. The room was shocked. At the end of the service, several guys decided to commit their lives to Jesus.

I was known as "Bible Answer Man" by local homeless guys. They would even call me that when they spotted me downtown. But after that service, several guys remarked to me, "I didn't know you were so tough, Bible Answer Man." I told them I was simply doing my job—which was to create a safe environment to discuss God, the Bible, and religion. I had taken a big risk by being very firm with the out-of-control man, but it was in a safe-ish environment, and I had knowledge of the situation, the people in the room, and what I would do if things escalated further.

My friend who was the night-shift supervisor—who had been homeless as a teenager, over ten years earlier—told me that my yelling back was the best thing I could have done. It helps that a little rage lives under the surface of my nicely pressed shirt, but the truth of the matter is that I still felt a little bad afterward—until a month later, in fact, when the guy who had yelled at me committed his life to Christ. He never asked me to forgive him, but I could see that he now liked me. Somewhere along the way, the very tough love had worked. I had been honest with him and the others in the room—and they respected that.

Just as establishing respect and trust is a necessary component of working with the homeless, so is the administration of tough love. Nevertheless, I can't stand fire-and-brimstone preaching to the homeless—I can't handle people telling them that they're bad or evil, or reminding them that they're sinners. "For heaven's sake," I always think when hearing that kind of preaching to the homeless. "These guys live on the street or in a mission; they know their lives are messed up."

My most effective ministry to the homeless has come when I answer their questions about God, the Bible, and religion honestly—and then remind them of Christ's redemption of my life and His belief in what they can be. Christ didn't come to show us that we're sinners—that was already done by the law, as Paul reminds us throughout Galatians. Jesus came to show God's belief in humanity—and to save us through His death and resurrection. (See, for example, John 3:17.) He boldly proclaims resurrection in our lives today, in this moment.

That is the kind of hope ministry we must have among all impoverished people. We must be brutally honest, but our focus must not be on people's faults—instead, it must be on the success God can offer. Remember, we are not above anyone in the eyes of God. The least important people in the eyes of the world are called the greatest in the kingdom of heaven. (See Luke 9:48.)

Couches Aren't Meant to Be Beds

It is very tempting to put a homeless person up in your house—don't do it, unless the Spirit tells you to do so.

> I spent years couch surfing—going from one friend's house to the next. This allowed for me to use the cash I had to buy the drugs and alcohol I was addicted to. Many of the people whose couches I slept on had no idea that I was an addict. I masked it well. If only they had cut me off sooner. I burned all of them eventually. But if they had simply kicked me out after a night, things would have been different. Maybe I would not have become more addicted. Maybe I would still have rights to see my kids.

When my rehabilitated friend Peter said these words, it completely transformed my perspective. I am not suggesting that you don't put someone up for the night, but I am suggesting that you place very clear limits on their stay—limits that you will enforce. It depends on how unstable the person staying with you is at that time. Could they possibly be harmful to the people in your home? If you can send people to your local mission instead, I recommend that. It would be tough love, but it would be more effective. Do you know how to diagnose all the spiritual, mental, and possibly addictive problems of your friend or acquaintance? A mission does. A true friend does what is best for the other person, and sometimes that means making hard decisions.

Of course, there are exceptions to this, such as a woman seeking refuge from an abusive husband; but again, be cautious that you don't create a dependent relationship. The only person we want people dependent on is Jesus. Also, make sure that if you are turning people away from the hospitality of your home, it is truly for *their* benefit, not because of sin or selfishness in *your* heart. I'm not giving you an excuse to be a miser here.

The best thing you can give any person, homeless or not, is the opportunity to improve themselves—to stand on their own two feet. That's what my friend Peter would tell you. You probably can't offer this on your own, but your local mission probably can.

Furthermore, I know that an opportunity to improve yourself works because of my experience with Sam. I met Sam when I was speaking one evening at our local mission—again in chapel. I had a longstanding tradition of recapping the service with the night-shift supervisors. But on this night, the night-shift supervisor wasn't in his office, so I just sat there until he returned. And then he brought Sam by and said, "John, Sam just got here. Can he hang out with you for a while?" (I later learned that the mission workers intended for me to chat with Sam for a while—believing that he would open up to me—but they didn't tell me that at the time. This is funny to me now, but it made me a little mad when I found out; yet, I would never take back that evening.)

I asked Sam to tell me about himself. I had learned from previous conversations with homeless people not to ask leading questions because, in the past, it had aggravated a few guys who became suspicious that I was an undercover cop. As I indicated earlier, many homeless people are leery of the police. Sam proceeded to tell me that he was fresh out of prison.

I never ask people what they did when they tell me they were incarcerated or arrested, but Sam volunteered it. (I recommend you keep my practice of not asking for information that isn't volunteered, as it can bias you and be rude.)

Sam had done some terrible things and told me that it was all due to his views of people with dark skin. I got uncomfortable, knowing that there were several African American and Hispanic men at the mission that night. He then told me about the redemption of Jesus—and how he had found Jesus in prison, in a chapel service. Upon his release, he had come to this mission, instead of going to his parents' house, because of its program; he wanted to be discipled. Somewhere along the way, he had become pen pals with a rehabilitated gang leader who had been through the same program.

Only God can transform a life like Sam's. And Sam still didn't like authority figures—again, like many homeless people—but he opened up to me because, apparently, my reputation had spread through the pen-pal letters. Among this small group of people, I had a little bit of fame as "Bible Answer Man who loves us, but takes no crap" or a more colorful version of that title—that's what my homeless friends would say, at least. (That is the only kind of fame I desire, and I pray that may always be the case.) The mission supervisors knew this—and lo and behold, God knew that I was meant to be there the night Sam rolled in.

As sad as it is to say, not everyone will be like Sam. Some people don't want help, and you have to realize that and accept it now. If someone doesn't want help, all you can do is pray for them. But for people like Sam, it is well worth the investment in their life. You never know how simply doing what God asks will transform lives.

TRULY LOVING BY FINDING THE RIGHT MINISTRY FOR YOU

I want to encourage you think about the issues that have been brought up throughout this book when deciding which ministry you want to partner with. Is the ministry or nonprofit focused on more than just putting out people's fires? Are they focused on fully developing people into who Jesus created them to be, living as Jesus intended them to live? Are they able to show you evidence of people overcoming both their spiritual and physical poverty through their work?

The Church as the Center of Alleviating Local Poverty

If you want to get involved with an organization, ask if that organization is already partnering with your church. And if they aren't working with your church, could they be? Could you facilitate that? Also, ask your pastor what your church is directly doing for those who are impoverished. Are they simply feeding people? Or are they teaching people how to put food on their own plates? Are they simply "teaching a man to fish" or walking with the man as he learns to fish?

Those of us who are church leaders must find out who we can partner with locally to make a drastic difference in our communities. And by partnerships, I mean relationships between nonprofits and churches, between churches and businesses, and between churches and churches— all with the focus of empowering locals to overcome, in a sustainable way, the issues their neighborhoods are facing. We should ask ourselves, "Would the community notice if we disappeared?"

Holistically Transforming Local Neighborhoods

In my opinion, all ideas about holistic community development must revolve around sustainable job creation (through things like microloans), meeting basic needs, creating churches (through church grants or other means), and discipleship (training). Partnership and transparency must be central values when doing so—all with a focus upon how Christ wants to empower local leaders to dream for their communities and take action.

Each of us must determine what work is actually effective—meaning that it is truly transforming lives.

I cannot emphasize enough that we need to keep the gospel at the center. Jesus did indeed come to save the lost, but He understood the full picture of a person's life. He understood they must be loved completely. And we must do the same. That means we have to be brutally honest about the efforts we're involved with. That means admitting that just because an effort makes us feel good doesn't necessarily make it right—or the most effective use of resources. Likewise, just because a method is logistically complicated doesn't necessarily make it wrong. We must always consider the results for the people we're seeking to empower. Are they being loved well? And if not, what can we do to change that?

TRULY LOVING PEOPLE GLOBALLY

Sometimes the best way to love our global neighbor is from afar, by serving with a nonprofit or ministry in the U.S. that works with the global poor. I regularly encourage people, as their first step, to join a volunteer staff or to intern. Some nonprofits, such as Jesus' Economy, even have completely remote teams—meaning that you can help empower the impoverished from anywhere in the world. This is an incredible way to gain experience and knowledge, while using your skills to better the world. Of course, you can always go to the developing world yourself, but before you do, read this.

Going to the Developing World

If you have the developing world on your mind and you would like to visit a place with extreme poverty, there are a few things you need to do first: pray and check your intentions. Are you really ready for what you will experience there? Are you ready to be open-minded with people from another culture and possibly another religion? Do you view yourself as more important/educated/experienced/privileged than the people you are visiting? Are you going as a tourist (to consume or take) or as a servant (to give back)? Make sure your intentions are pure.

If you decide to go to the places on your heart, don't go and do something *for* people—do something *with* them. Go and observe people. Ask them nonjudgmental (open) questions. Have a conversation with locals. Consider what they're really saying.

When you go to the developing world, do whatever you can to make sure you journey with the right people—those who know what they're doing and are very experienced. Remember that you are representing Jesus and your home country. Leave a positive impression.

Traveling in the developing world can be extremely dangerous. And if you're not prepared emotionally and spiritually, you may have a slight breakdown. You may find that you are not quite as strong as you thought you were—spiritually, emotionally, and physically. The journey will be a challenge and you need to be ready for it. (Please read this paragraph again, because it's a serious consideration.)

What Is Your Goal?

I think one of the best things foreigners can do when traveling to the developing world is to spend time in communities just listening and talking with leaders—shadowing leaders who are passionate about the gospel in their community. Learn how leaders who are transforming lives are accomplishing their work. This will help you understand how you can get involved and where to get involved. But remember to keep your advice to yourself unless asked to share. They know the issues that need to be dealt with far better than you do, because they live those issues every day. It is your job to understand how you can help *them* accomplish the work. It's okay to offer your skills, but don't force yourself upon a leader or a community.

A good way to approach this is to be clear about expectations. Ask your hosts, "Is there anything I should know? Is there anything I should say or shouldn't say, anything I should do or shouldn't do?" Simply naming the potential difficulties and discussing them can address cross-cultural conflict, which is a very real thing. You can also say things like, "By being here, I just want to listen and experience life with you. If I can be of any help while I'm here, just say the word. Also, feel free to explain culture to me because I want to learn to honor the people we visit." If you have other expectations, such as a desire to work together, name that too: "My hope is that I will be able to work alongside you in addressing the needs of the community." Then ask open questions. The reality of the situation almost always presents itself if you ask good questions and listen intently.

Also remember that it is not a community leader's job to entertain you during your stay in their country. This goes back to the difference between being a tourist and being a servant. You are there to serve them and to be as little a burden as possible. This may mean arranging for your own transportation or lodging, finding your own meals, and generally being willing to help out with whatever is needed. Don't expect a car service or a place to stay. Don't expect a nonprofit leader to wait on you or give you their devoted attention. They are busy people who are often tapped out emotionally and physically by the strains of living in poverty. You are there to blend in—and to alleviate their burdens, not create more of them.

Letting Jesus Do the Toughest Work

I cannot emphasize enough how much gospel-centered ministry must be our focus. If we remove Jesus from the equation of helping the impoverished, we take out the component that will be the key to overcoming poverty itself. Water wells, medical clinics, and microloans are all good things—but without Jesus involved, we will miss out on changing the root cause of poverty: spiritual depravity.

How is it that Christians could possibly believe that a very deep-rooted problem could be overcome without Christ? Why would we ever remove Christ from anything? Jesus wants to be involved in all parts of our work. Now, I'm not suggesting that non-Christian organizations are somehow failing or lacking. I believe that they play a very important role in our world. But what I am saying is that, when possible, we should incorporate the gospel in word and deed. We want to see people free—do we not? And if we want to see the captives set free, then we must show them that Jesus can set them free. (See, for example, Luke 4:18.)

TRULY LOVING THROUGH SHORT-TERM MISSIONS

To be frank, I've always had issues with short-term missions. I have often wondered why we would spend thousands of dollars to visit a community, become a burden to them by suddenly requiring them to find food and shelter for a huge group, then leave without really doing much at all. It seemed to me that we would be better off sending the money we would have spent traveling there directly to the community to use on projects they care about. That said, at one point when I was in northeast India, there was a short-term mission group present. Their presence appeared to bless the nonprofit they were serving, as well as the people in the villages they visited. It seemed as if outsiders coming to help affirmed how valued the people were in God's eyes. ("If someone came all the way from [fill in the blank] to see me, I must not be forgotten by God.")

Since that experience, I have realized that it is not my place to judge those who feel called to short-term missions.

Check Your Motives

As with any work among the impoverished, as you consider going on a short-term mission trip, ask yourself, "What is my motivation?" Also ask yourself, "Do I really believe God is calling me to this place?" If He is, then you must go. If He is not, then you should stay home. It is that simple.

If God is calling you to go on a short-term mission trip, then make sure you understand the place's culture and customs. Do whatever you can to shed assumptions about the region you are going to. In addition, make sure you understand the groundwork already in place that you will be building upon: "Who is there and what are they doing? And how long have they been there?"

Above all, it is absolutely critical that short-term mission groups listen closely and intently to the local leaders whom they are supporting. Because after the group leaves, that leader will be left to deal with whatever legacy the short-term group has left—whether good or bad. Always remember that, depending on your actions and behavior, you have the ability to either show people the renewal of Jesus or to ruin any witness a long-term missionary or local indigenous leader had with their community.

Once You're on the Ground

Once you're on the ground, ask the local leader what they need and what you can do to assist them. Submit yourself to their authority. Use the same guidelines as were presented in the previous chapter. Show respect. Remember that you are a guest. (And remember that you have the potential to make a mess—literal or figurative—that will have to be cleaned up when you leave.)

If you're costing a local ministry resources, be sure that you offer to pay your own way—ideally, you will have this conversation before you go. Consider the burden you may be placing on them and respond in kind. Note for them how grateful you are for their hospitality, and state that you would like to repay the kindness in whatever way you can. At this point, they will likely tell you if and how they want you to repay them, but culturally, the response will vary. Understanding the cultural issues is hugely important. Some cultures feel that it will dishonor you to ask for money in exchange for their hospitality. The golden rule applies here: treat your host as you would want to be treated. But also remember the power disparity: you are probably much wealthier than your host and could very well be burdening them financially. If it is possible to help with this burden, while honoring your host, do so. For example, you could offer to pay for meals, saying something like, "To thank you for your hospitality, please let me pay. It would be my honor."

Honor is a key word here. Honor and shame are a major part of most cultures in the global East and South. You never want to do something that could cause your host to feel shame (such as making them feel that they are unable to provide for you). And if you preface your desire to do something for your host in terms of *your* honor—"it would be *my* honor"—they will usually defer and allow you to carry part of the financial burden of your visit. However, in this regard, be sure to always receive hospitality, too, meaning a meal, offers of tea, whatever lodging accommodations are provided, and so forth. Saying no can be a great dishonor.

In addition to these cautions, be sure that you are self-sufficient during your stay by doing research on the types of items you will need to bring, the immunization shots you will need to have had, and similar factors.

Always consider if you are doing something that may cause the host ministry harm or weaken the effectiveness of their message. Have you thought through all the ramifications of your actions?

This might seem like too much to think about each moment, and it may be, but if you have thought about things ahead of time, your training will kick in. The real key here is to submit yourself to local leadership and ask questions if you don't understand something—following the local's lead. And above all, pray before doing anything. Before opening your mouth, pray. Before opening your wallet, pray. Definitely before getting on a plane, pray.

How Will You Report What You've Seen?

Additionally, think about how you will report what you learn on your trip. And each step along the way, consider what God is doing. Journaling can be a great assistance in this process. A journal can help you to recall specific moments, but it can also help you to prayerfully reflect upon your experiences.

At the end of your trip, force yourself to write a report. This will help you process your experience and learn what you needed to learn. It will also help you share your experiences with others.

Make it a regular habit to recall the stories of how God worked in your life and the lives of the people you were serving. It will encourage you and others when you share these stories, and it could inspire people to make a change in their own lives. It could be how God shows them a part of Himself.

In Case You're Now Worried

Know that the Holy Spirit will guide you. You don't need to think through each and every situation ahead of time—and you won't be able to anyway. If you are discerning, you will know what works and doesn't work through the Spirit's guidance and the direction of the leaders around you.

Take courage. If God has called you, He will provide the way and the means.

TRULY LOVING BY CHANGING YOUR GIVING HABITS

Now that you have decided to not just hand people money, one of the most difficult situations you will face is what to do when people ask you for it.

When I Failed to Empower a Fellow Church Member

In the church plant I used to help lead, there was a lady who always seemed to be in a crisis situation. If I had known what I know now, I probably would have helped her address the reasons why her crisis situations existed—but I didn't.

Our church would listen each week as she would tell us about the difficulties she was facing as she moved from one crisis to the next. It was sad and painful. It made us all feel bad that we had so much and she had so little.

What I didn't know until later, however, was that I wasn't the only one who had been giving her money now and again—most people in our small church had been giving her money, food, rides, and more every month. At one point, I asked around and calculated how much we all had given her, and it was a substantial amount of money—per month, it was more than most of us would ever make in our paychecks. She was a student with no children, living in subsidized housing, who didn't work—not because she couldn't, but because she was too busy, got laid off, or some other reason. The situation did not make sense.

Our church leadership team agreed that this was not healthy and that we needed to find a way to help her move from crisis to stability. Some people in our church had already been coaching her on her resume and cover letter writing, as well as proofreading her resume and cover letters, but by then, it was too late. The final shoe dropped when a friend of hers, someone she lovingly called her "bank," tried to commit suicide. She'd had no idea that her friend was even depressed.

In all, our church tried to stabilize the woman's situation for her for nine months, until her landlord finally kicked her out. A family from the church gave her temporary housing and sent her to a financial counselor, who eventually told her that she needed to move back home (where she had a bigger network of friends and family), get a job in her hometown, and start fresh.

What would have happened if we had stopped the enabling before she was evicted? Would she have ended up back home sooner? Would she have ended up on her feet? What if we had directed her to local resources for empowerment instead of thinking we knew what to do? What if we had established boundaries about what we considered a crisis situation instead of determining it on the fly? What if we had trained our church members on what constitutes a crisis situation—and the need to pool resources to handle it, not handle it as individuals—and then acted in accordance with our standards? What if we had actually been handling the situation as the New Testament church handled similar situations?

As a church leadership team, we had failed to initiate a program for helping the impoverished, and in the process, someone's situation became unbearable for all of us.

The Keys to Helping a Church Member Overcome Poverty

Just like ministry to the homeless, the first key to tackling the issue of someone at church asking you for money is to know the resources available locally. Your church also has to have a plan in place—which we will discuss later.

Know what the game plan is before the situation occurs, and act in accordance with your training and plan. But above that, consider walking alongside the person. Rather than just giving money, why not give work/tasks in exchange for money? It is empowering for a person to earn what they are given, even if what they are able to give back is exponentially smaller than what they receive.

As Christians, we often feel stuck between the balance of giving freely and requiring something in return. God has given freely to us. He has given us His grace and redemption from sins, free of charge. While we can do nothing to earn this grace, remember that He does ask something from us: our obedience, faithfulness, devotion, and love. This doesn't earn us salvation—that's a free gift—but it does show God we care about our relationship with Him.

We should use the same model when helping other people. First, think of how you can show grace and love to another person. We love God because He first loved us. (See 1 John 4:19.) Being there for someone, in relationship, is the first step. We need to take God's love and pass it on to others. But it should be done in the context of *authentic* relationship, like the one we have with God. That takes us to the second step for interpersonal interactions.

It is in the context of true love and compassion that we help others. Not to get rid of people. Not to make their problems "go away" so we can keep living our lives. But so that we can all be truly transformed in Christ, free of sins that weigh us down. This means that it's okay for you to have expectations of other people. God has expectations for all of us. It's okay to expect people to *want to* do something about their own problems. You should not be "fixing" someone's problem, but empowering them to fix it. And you should *expect* that *they* will do so. So get involved in the empowering aspect by asking solution-focused questions and executing the solutions your church has already agreed upon.

Also note that you give money personally to your church (and other organizations) so that they can help people in these kinds of situations. They can evaluate the situation as an impartial team, with wisdom and discernment. That should free you up to be an *authentic* friend, not someone's personal "bank."

TRULY LOVING VIA YOUR CHURCH

Now that you have read most of this book, you may have some frustrations with the way your church is approaching poverty. If you feel that part of your church—or your church in general—is dealing with poverty incorrectly, you need to address the issue head-on but lovingly and with humility. Remember, we are all still in a learning process. It will be difficult, but worth it.

Start with a Face-to-Face Conversation

When correcting a problem, you should always begin with a conversation—preferably with the person in charge of poverty alleviation or missions efforts in your church or another leader who is actively involved in these programs. You can start by inviting them out for coffee to tell them what you're learning or by suggesting books you've read that they might like. (Now, I once had a pastor joke with me that people who disagree with him usually hand him books, so be careful that your decision to give someone a book is not passive-aggressive.) Of course, the latter method only works if the person you're talking to is a reader—and learns that way.

If your approach to talk with the individual doesn't work, then it is time to bring the problem up with a leader who has more authority (such as an elder at your church), but do so with all parties present, including the person you are disagreeing with. If the problem is with the approach of the church overall, then it is best to invite the pastor to be there.

Get Directly Involved

Of course, you can almost always get directly involved in making changes in your church. Begin by developing a plan to revise the way your church approaches poverty. The best way to start is to evaluate the assets (or strengths) that your local community—meaning the neighborhood, town, or county—possesses, and try to develop a plan around how you can use those assets to combat poverty issues. Think about how you can create positive change in your community and empower others to do the same.

Making a Community Development Plan

While formulating any community development plan, ask the following questions:

+ How will it help people outside your church overcome poverty?

+ What are the specific needs of your community?

+ What are the strengths in your community that you can use to meet those needs?

+ Will the plan focus on neighborhoods or will it be a city- or county-wide effort?

+ Who will direct the execution of the plan?

+ Who are the stakeholders—the leaders in your community—that you need to have involved each step along the way?

+ How can you get people from your community involved—working *with* them, rather than *for* them?

Your plan should also be goal focused. But these goals should revolve around relationships. What is your goal for your community, and what is your community's collective goal for itself? How can Jesus be involved in the middle of it all to make a difference in people's lives? Remember that as a representative of Christ, your ultimate goal is to share about Jesus and have people experience Him in tangible ways—so, how will your plan make new disciples of Jesus?

By answering these questions and thinking through these issues, you will start to develop a plan. And then, you will be able to effectively and sustainably alleviate poverty in your community through creating jobs, planting churches, meeting basic needs, and training people. I believe these four components are pillars of truly loving people—they're pillars of overcoming physical and spiritual poverty.

Ensuring Your Plan Also Deals with Crisis Situations

In addition to your community development plan, think about how you can create a plan for how your church handles the needs of people asking for assistance. What constitutes a crisis and what doesn't? What structure is in place to review the need? And how can this structure be efficient and quick?

Often, these situations will need a solution (or at least an answer) within twenty-four hours. For example, someone may need a bus ticket for later that afternoon, or they may be getting evicted that day. The church needs to set up strict criteria for who gets aid and how it's given out. (This is basically what Paul tells Timothy to do in 1 Timothy 5:1–18.) Responsible generosity is the key here. As members of the church, we don't steward funds for the purpose of hoarding them for ourselves. Instead, we see the money as given *by* God, *for* God's work. That requires extreme generosity and a good knowledge of the situation at hand to make sure we're being as responsible as possible.

Ask (and answer) these questions: What process will people go through to request assistance? How will they learn of the process? Who will they hear from? Who will follow up with them? It takes more time and effort to do things this way, but consider the consequences of not doing so: wasting thousands of donated dollars, allowing people to be trapped in sin and poverty cycles, and possibly giving someone a tool to harm themselves or others.

Although I have given much cautionary advice, remember that every action must also be done in prayer. If God leads you to give in the moment, without regard for where the money or items are going, then you must do so. However, knowing that He is the God of relationships and community, it is certain that engaging in community with someone is the approach He will ask you to take with most everyone you meet.

He desires to meet their immediate spiritual needs as well as their immediate physical needs.

Once You Have a Plan

Once you develop your plan, begin to execute it like any other business situation. Determine the funds you will need and request those from your community or from outside organizations (or businesses). This can allow for you to do something substantial and incredible for the world without even having to leave your own backyard. For some communities, the emphasis will need to be more on alleviating physical poverty; for others, the emphasis will need to be more on addressing spiritual poverty. It all depends on the needs of the particular community. But remember to not separate physical needs from spiritual needs—they are interwoven.

You will find that having a plan to overcome spiritual and physical poverty in your community will give you a new passion for life. And through your efforts, you will see lives transformed. This is not really about the project—this is about the people you're serving. There is nothing more important than relationships.

But What If My Church Isn't Willing to Change?

Community development plans can create unity in your church. They can create unity between your church and other churches. And they can create unity among your neighborhood, city, and county. They can help your community overcome difficulties and lead to lives being renewed. But the reality is that some people will still not embrace community development—or even the idea of it.

If your local church is unwilling to embrace community development, do your best to offer new hope and vision to your community yourself. Meanwhile, try to help your church community see a new reality. Be sure that you use your knowledge out of compassion. Do not use it as an excuse to create disunity.

Our churches need us to serve them—and sometimes this means a long road of loving difficult people into loving others better and more holistically. We are not meant to be served or entertained by the church. We are meant to take part in it, as integral members of the body of Christ.

We don't protect the church by keeping others out or ignoring them. We invite the people on the outside (literally and figuratively) to come in and join us, as Jesus did.

The church has no walls. Its members share a bond in Christ that stretches to every community across the globe. The more we see ourselves as interconnected, the faster we can change our world for Jesus.

TRULY LOVING SOMEONE IN THE MISSION FIELD

Nearly all of us who are Christians know someone who is serving Christ by being in the mission field. How can we best love both local missionaries to their own people and missionaries who have moved to other countries to serve Jesus?

Prayer: It's Simple and Never Goes out of Style

One of the best things you can do for people in the mission field is to pray for them. It's an incredible way to come alongside them in their journey. I encourage you to keep a prayer list of people around the globe—and to commit to praying for them regularly. You can even set a specific time on your calendar that you do so, to ensure that you don't forget.

Encouragement

Giving fiscally to someone's efforts for God's kingdom is a fantastic way to help, but sending encouraging messages is also a great way to give someone the extra energy they may stand in need of. You would be amazed how many missionaries send out reports to people and never hear anything back. The missionary reports about people coming to Christ—or overcoming physical poverty—are incredible, and yet, more often than not, missionaries never hear from their supporters after they show them what God is doing. Missionaries need to hear from their supporters as much as their supporters need to hear from them. They are often lonely and feel isolated. So write an encouraging message to someone in the mission field today.

Consider asking someone in the mission field what they need and how you can help them. Ask them what's going on in their life and what it's like on the ground. If you know someone in the mission field who isn't offering reports that articulate these things, encourage them to do so. It will help them rally support around their cause.

Many missionaries also go for great lengths of time without being invited to speak at a church or event. You can create opportunities for missionaries to share their message at your church. This is not only encouraging, but it also opens up doors of support for them.

Consider the Resources at Your Disposal

You can also consider using simple things, like your birthday or an event, to make a difference in someone's life. There are organizations that offer birthday and event dedications to help those in poverty—where you can designate your birthday for a specific cause, and people can give to the cause instead of getting you gifts (or paying admission to the event). This is a great way to raise awareness about what's going on around the globe, as well as raise funds. (Jesus' Economy offers such a program and so do several other organizations.)

The Old Fridge Photo

It may seem kind of old-school, but putting the photo of a missionary on your fridge can make a huge difference. First, it helps you remember to pray for them. Second, people who come to your house will ask you about the photo, and it will give you the opportunity to tell them about the great work that missionary is doing.

Remember that you can be an incredible encouragement to those who are in the field working hard for God's kingdom. In addition, keep in mind that few of us have it as hard as the persecuted church—we should be regularly lifting these believers up in our prayers. (You can learn about the efforts of the persecuted church from organizations such as International Christian Response.) Let's be grateful that we have the freedom to come alongside those serving Jesus around the globe and show them our support.

TRULY LOVING WITH YOUR MONEY

We all like to get the biggest bang for our buck. And I believe it is good stewardship to ensure that we do so.

Understanding the Organization's Purpose

When you evaluate the effectiveness of an organization you're considering donating to, the most important thing you can do is to understand their stated purpose. This may be found right at the beginning of their bylaws. These bylaws should be online. And if they're not, at least the stated mission of the organization will be somewhere on their "About" page or elsewhere on their website. When you understand the organization's purpose, you can decide if you are passionate about their cause. If you are not passionate about what they are doing, you should probably stop your analysis at this stage and look for another organization to support.

The Fiscal Evaluation

The next key would be to find the organization's most recent annual report. If they don't have it online, call to ask for a copy of it. (Any organization that is hesitant to give this to you probably has some serious issues.) Inside the report should be a section that shows you the breakdown of how the organization's financials were used during the last year, by percentages. The first thing you're looking for here is how much went to administration and how much went to fundraising—these are two areas of expenses usually considered overhead. However, understand that some organizations must have high administration because of the type of work they do—that is, it could be very difficult to work in the regions they're working in. They could also have a small staff and thus their executive costs—which all get rolled into administration—will seem high. There are different views about how much should be spent on fundraising and administration, but generally you want to see these costs being less than 20 percent—25 percent at a maximum. Ten percent administration is considered very good, and 5 percent is considered incredible.

It's also important to understand how an organization comes up with their fiscal percentage figures. For example, some organizations can falsely appear better than others because of the type of work they do. An aid organization can look much better on paper than a community development organization, because they receive many in-kind gifts (donated goods)—this raises the amount of money or goods put toward projects and thus makes the percentage toward administration seem smaller.

Checks and Balances

When evaluating a nonprofit, you're also looking for checks and balances. Is there a strong board of directors whose members are unbiased—meaning that they do not receive pay for their work? Is the treasurer qualified? Is the CEO qualified? Do they have a regular financial audit or review?

Of course, there are also independent bodies that evaluate organizations, but keep in mind that a young organization will not have the ability to have the same kind of independent analysis of their practices—because it will be cost prohibitive or because they're still a start-up. (Independent financial reviews cost at least $5,000 and audits are usually at least $10,000.) To compensate, young organizations should be financially transparent—as, in my opinion, all organizations should be.

The Effectiveness of the Work

Don't just be concerned about the percentages. Your chief concern when evaluating an organization should be the effectiveness of their work. Can they provide examples of how their work is truly and sustainably helping other people? Ask yourself, "Is the work helping people overcome poverty, or is it simply addressing the symptom of poverty?" and

"Which organization does the community really need in this moment?" (Obviously, if the community has suffered devastation from a hurricane or flood, choosing not to give to an aid organization that is bringing relief to the area is ridiculous. Emergency aid is what the community needs most at such times.)

You will also want to understand an organization's model. Can the organization provide you with a full explanation of what they do and why they do it? Are they available for questions about the model and their efforts? Will they answer your questions sufficiently if you ask them?

The Principles of the Organization

Consider the principles of the organization: Are they stated somewhere on their website, and what are they? For example, there are several organizations now—including Jesus' Economy—that are using solely a restricted-fund model, in which donors designate precisely how their money is used. When a donor chooses not to designate funds, it is put in the general account and used for projects only. Administrative funds are raised separately. There are advantages and disadvantages to this model. Again, transparency is the key.

It is my belief that, as a donor, you have the full right to ask organizations any and all questions—there's no need for you to hesitate to do so. Any organization that is unwilling or hesitant to be transparent—and cannot provide a good reason for why they are withholding information—is, frankly, not worth your money.

TRULY LOVING BY EXPANDING YOUR CHURCH'S EFFORTS

Like individual donors, churches often wonder how they can best use their money and resources to overcome poverty. Here are some very practical pointers that build on the tips for creating a community development plan that I mentioned earlier.

Partnership for Local Poverty Alleviation

I cannot recommend enough that your church consider partnering with another church near you. I also cannot recommend enough that your church consider partnering with other organizations. There is too much duplication of effort going on in our communities and around the globe. We are wasting time, energy, and assets that Jesus has given us. We can stop doing so today by engaging in partnerships.

For local poverty alleviation, the church plant I am part of asked neighborhood folks, local leaders (including school principals), local artists, and government officials how we could work alongside them to overcome poverty. We then used this data to create a plan together. We invited key people to have a meeting about their neighborhood and started to develop plans for things that we could do together to make it a better place to live. We also got involved in some of the nitty-gritty, and dirty, work of simply serving our neighbors who needed assistance (for example, taking them to appointments or cleaning their homes).

Eventually, a group of local leaders voted on how we could collectively use our resources toward the betterment of the community. We developed

a plan together for how we would help our church—and the community—
be more effective.

We also partner with other local organizations to support them with
volunteer labor, in order to execute projects, and, even at times, fiscally.

I'm not saying that everything we do at our church plant is effective,
but I do believe that it is working overall because we were the first church
to get traction in the neighborhood. Also, at the end of the day, our plan
was executed out of obedience to what we believed Christ had called us to
do—and that's what really matters most.

Partnership for Global Poverty Alleviation

On the partnership level, your church may also want to consider
working with a global organization. This could happen through your church
deciding to give fiscally to a ministry that is effectively empowering people
in the developing world—straight out of your budget. Or, it could mean
doing something like what our church did, which was to give our every
tenth offering to an outside organization, with the leadership team deciding
who that organization would be (rotating through several different ones).

Your church could also consider holding an event to raise funds for a
developing-world church (or churches)—or another cause you're passionate about. Likewise, your church could support missionaries by hosting
them for fundraising events.

No matter what you do, I want to encourage you to get involved
missionally by supporting organizations that are already working in areas
that you're passionate about. We need more partnerships.

I have found that many churches don't partner with other organizations or other churches because they're concerned about their church not
having enough money or losing focus. I believe that both of these ideas are
erroneous and that the opposite will actually happen—the global focus
will enhance the credibility of your church and inspire people to engage
more, not less, with your efforts.

TRULY LOVING THROUGH YOUR WORK

It's easier than ever to truly love people through your work. You can love your co-workers like you would truly love a neighbor. You can help create jobs in your business. You can inspire others in your company to give to a cause, and, if you're a business owner, you can use your company to fund life transformation.

I often wonder, what would the world be like if we could redeem capitalism—so that the end result of our efforts was always the creation of jobs and the empowerment of the impoverished? We could potentially see a beautiful change in our economy and in our world.

Nonprofits are making it easier than ever for companies to help the impoverished. Innovative nonprofits are offering a wide variety of ways to adopt their cause and offer matching grants. This sort of grassroots marketing effort for alleviating poverty is becoming very effective throughout the U.S.; I think it will one day be the norm. It creates great PR for a business and can really help transform communities.

Simple Ideas for Businesses

Your business can do simple things to truly love others. For example, a local coffee shop in my hometown chooses a particular day to give everyone a free coffee who donates five dollars to a local charity. And the reward system works—people give more than the cost of the coffee, so that a substantial amount is raised. From everything I can tell, they have more business on that day than other days too. Many companies are also offering people the opportunity to donate to a cause at checkout. One common method is to ask the customer to round up their order to the nearest dollar; the company then donates the difference to a nonprofit. This well demonstrates how many people agreeing to a small generous act can create positive change. The "win" is in the aggregate.

Your business could also consider doing something like hosting an event where a percentage of the proceeds goes to charity. Or, you might choose a product that you sell, and designate a percentage of the sales of that product for charity. Or, for every product purchased, you could do something significant in the developing world (see the ONE Campaign for an example). Many big companies are using this technique to boost their company image and to boost overall sales. I love it when businesses or groups get involved in doing something for a cause. It makes me more likely to want to buy from them (or continue to buy from them).

While I do have my hesitancies about how particular campaigns can easily "market" poverty, I'm always grateful when money goes to helping the impoverished. So my big caution for companies is to be careful *how* you talk about poverty. This means to be transparent about *what* you're giving, *why* you're doing it, and *who* is benefiting. If your company is getting more benefit than the impoverished, that's a problem. If you're using the story of someone's poverty to make a sale, that's a problem too. Considering basic human dignity—how people are represented—isn't difficult; you just have to stop and think about motivations and what your marketing is really saying.

When Your Company Thinks of Buying, Think Fair Trade

It's surprisingly rare for a company to consider how what they *already do* can create jobs for the impoverished globally. For example, is there something your company regularly buys (like pencils, notepads, or coffee) that could be supplied via a fair trade company? Could your next promotional product be a handmade item from the developing world? What about your next company gift?

Many fair trade organizations offer personalized branding on fair trade goods—such as journals. You can get quality, exploitation-free items with your company's logo on them. This is a great alternative to the typical promotional products, since it leaves both a lasting impression about what your company represents and ensures that jobs are created for the impoverished globally.

Companies can also make a positive difference by critically examining how their supply chain might involve the exploitation of labor. This is simpler than it sounds. Ask your vendors where they get their products made and how the people they work with are paid. If you don't get straight answers, that's a sign that a change needs to take place.

Use Your Skills

All of us have skills we use every day to earn a living, raise a family, complete an educational degree, pursue a particular hobby, and so forth. Now, we have the opportunity to pass along a number of these skills to people worldwide. Due to greater Internet access in developing-world economies, many of these skills can even be shared online, without requiring travel. Whatever your skills, they don't have to be revolutionary or completely unique to you. They can be something that seems simple yet can have a profound impact on the recipient. Here are some examples I've personally witnessed of people using their skills for the good of the impoverished and marginalized, whether in their home country or abroad:

- An agricultural farmer traveled to Africa and set up an example crop for the village, using modern farming techniques designed for arid environments. The crop produced double the yield of the locals' previous method and they were convinced to use the new method.

- A fashion designer from New York moved to Rwanda to help women learn how to make designer clothing from their local textiles.

- A retired teacher met with a Ugandan immigrant once a day at the library to teach him to read English.

- A man fixed his spare car for a Ghanaian immigrant who was riding his bike thirty miles to work every day.

- A grandmother taught a young mother living at a halfway house how to make healthy freezer meals for her kids.

+ A photo editor created better photography for a nonprofit's website.

+ A web developer designed custom code to fix an ongoing problem with a nonprofit's website and built a website for a church focused on serving the marginalized and those yet to know Jesus.

+ A college student built a database for a nonprofit that allowed them to find more fair trade artisans to empower.

+ A group of men helped a disabled veteran put siding on his house.

+ A stay-at-home mom moonlighted as an executive assistant for a nonprofit to ensure that donors, customers, and developing-world partners were well cared for.

+ A salesperson used his skills to help coordinate new partnerships for a ministry that serves the impoverished and unreached people groups globally.

+ An extreme extravert used her jovial personality to get people to community events and spread the message of how best to help the impoverished and bring the gospel to the unreached.

These are just examples I have personally witnessed. I have heard of many, many more. If you have a skill in anything at all, it could be used to absolutely change someone's life.

Your company can even pool its employees' skills (on a volunteer basis) to offer specialized services to nonprofits. You could provide a service to an organization by simply offering, once a month, for part of a day or a full day, the use of the team you lead. This is also a great way for your team to build community together and to grow. Collaborating together on a worthy project to help people in need can instill a sense of purpose and creativity.

Put simply, try operating with the idea of an economy of abundance in mind. Think about how your skills and the skills of those you work with could be used for the good of other people. Think about the assets God has given you. Think of yourself as part of Jesus' economy. Then, be on the lookout for ways you can use your skills to help others today.

EPILOGUE: NEVER STOP TRULY LOVING

It is easy to lose heart when there is so much work to be done in our world: so many to lead to Jesus and so many to empower out of poverty. We may look at the situation and ask ourselves, "What good can we actually do?" But, in such moments, there is encouragement just around the corner.

Whenever I hear a story of an individual in poverty truly being helped—meaning someone working with them to empower them toward sustainable living—I am joyous. It resonates and reverberates in my heart. I believe this is the case because it is a sign of God at work; it is a reminder to me that He is overturning the evil, disorder, and pain in our world and replacing it with goodness and love. In those moments, I see Jesus' economy.

I want you to think about this concept—the idea of people everywhere overcoming spiritual and physical poverty. Think about it each and every time you consider helping people in need. Try to feel it in your bones.

I also want you to imagine what life is like for the impoverished and unreached. Consider the difference it makes when someone shows them love and the joy it brings. Then, consider how it makes you feel when someone truly sees you and empowers you. When they really ask you how you're feeling and validate your importance to God. Place yourself for a moment in that position of vulnerability and picture how different you feel after someone acts in accordance with God's will to bring *you* love and goodness, and empowers *you* to have a sustainable livelihood.

But perhaps there is another way for you to visualize this. Think back upon a situation that made you feel helpless and distraught. Remember how you eventually made your way out of it. Recall the people who loved you in those dark moments and walked with you as you moved forward. Consider how God brought you to Himself.

Now, go and do likewise for other people.

Love God. Love other people. Offer hope. Be encouraged. Don't lose heart. Together, we can make the world a better place.

Jesus' economy is based on self-sacrifice.

Jesus' currency is love.

May that idea change your life and our world.

ACKNOWLEDGMENTS

Just as the nonprofit Jesus' Economy is Jesus', so is this book. Where I have erred, may God be gracious and allow me to correct my ways and words. Where what I have written aligns with God's vision for the world, may the words become actions and change lives. May all glory and honor be given to God alone.

As you've probably realized, this book is deeply personal. It almost feels like giving a part of myself to you, the reader. Jesus' economy is an idea I aim to live; by God's grace, it has become an embodied reality in my life. I pray that it may become even more so as I learn to use the currency of love and live the economy of self-sacrifice. It is my hope and prayer that God would do the same for you.

Like any spiritual journey, the journey of living Jesus' economy has involved many guides. Let me take a moment to share with you about a few of them.

The first guide I call "the voice." This is a term the romantics used to describe the primary person they wrote to and who they always heard in their mind when writing. For me, that is my wife, Kalene. She is often the first audience of my words and the one who filters out all the terrible ideas. So you should thank her too. Kalene is also the voice that points me back to Jesus, time and time again. She is my partner in entrepreneurship, ministry, and life. Living with a writer is hard enough—they are often caffeinated narcissists—but Kalene also literally joins in the journey of this story. She is living the journey of Jesus' economy. She is my Ozean Augen, my Ginevra, and a saint.

I also have other colleagues in arms on this path. Via the nonprofit Jesus' Economy, I am blessed to have many people walk into the unknown with me. The Jesus' Economy Board of Directors has walked with Kalene and me as we have collectively made impossible ideas reality. Only by the grace of God has this been the case. The Jesus' Economy volunteer staff has self-sacrificially given for this cause, as they too have embodied these ideas. Whenever I have been in need of inspiration, I have not had to look far. As I have shared much of this book on the Jesus' Economy blog, our team has helped hone it, share it, and inspire me to dig deeper. And now we get to see God use these words to fund His work through JesusEconomy.org.

On dusty roads in India, I had other guides. Biju Thomas, his family, and other incredible leaders at Transformation India Movement allowed me to shadow them. Through their pioneering efforts to bring the gospel to the unreached and empower the impoverished, I learned much of what I know. They taught me how to truly love my global neighbors. They also inspired me to live self-sacrificially and to truly believe in what can be. This is why many of my stories in this book are their stories, which I was graciously invited into.

Back in the U.S., part of my journey starts before I was a thought. My parents, Vickie and Leon Barry, pulled themselves out of poverty with grit and hard work and, thus, gave me stable economic ground on which to start my life. Kalene's parents, Marty and Cheryl Mitchell, also acted as guides to hospitality, as they not only provided for Kalene but also provided a home for us as we launched a new phase of Jesus' Economy.

There are also all those people who don't know they are guides, but are. Robert (Bob) Lupton inspired me to write the theological backing for what he had already found to be true through experience. Eugene and Minhee Cho inspired Kalene and me to take the leap to be founders and to live self-sacrificially. Sunday Bobai Agang, Nathan Byrd, and Eng Hoe, Lim helped guide my thinking on the mentality of poverty and showed me how Jesus can heal that too.

Then there are those guides we call editors. *Relevant* magazine gave me the opportunity to publish early portions of this book as articles on RelevantMagazine.com, specifically, slightly different (and shorter) versions of "Jesus Will Shock You" and "The First Christian Entrepreneur." The editors at Salem Web Network and Red Letter Christians regularly featured my ideas and made suggestions for improvements and new topics.

And the team at Whitaker House ultimately made this book a reality—and much better.

On the streets of the City of Subdued Excitement, the team at Lighthouse Mission Ministries taught me how to truly love the homeless. The team at The Table taught me how to live as a missionary right in my hometown. And collectively, the two teams helped me to live Jesus' currency of love.

My spiritual guides came in accountability partners and relationships. Aaron Walters, J.D. Elgin, and Paul Foth each told me what to read next, how I'm *not* living like Jesus, and *how I can* live like Jesus. They said the hard words in my life that I desperately needed to hear and prayed for me, even when I no longer believed in myself.

I have also had the uncommon experience of having "speaking guides." A group of speech therapists taught me to speak as a child. And then there was that day the guide Gabriel showed up, to tell me to use my voice. You all gave me a voice, so that I can now give a voice to the voiceless.

There are people who believe in God's work *in you*. I know that I do. May Jesus be your ultimate guide, as He has been mine.

BOOKS YOU PROBABLY SHOULD READ

I'm glad you're a reader. I know this to be true because you're reading these words. I'm a reader too. While it's often hard to quantify how ideas influence us and where these ideas eventually resurface, I know the following set of books greatly influenced my writing of *Jesus' Economy*. It is the ideas of these authors that operate in the background of my writing.

It's difficult to know if you will have the same epiphany moments I did when reading these works, but I hope that the combination of books listed here will cause you to think differently. I hope that in reading further on this topic, you will become a little wiser, a little cleverer, and more emotionally attuned to the needs of our world. I hope the writings of other authors will help you see more clearly how to live Jesus' economy in all aspects of life.

The Short List of Books I Regularly Recommend

Seriously, You Have to Read This

The Bible. Pick a readable translation and get on a consistent reading plan where you regularly read the Bible in its entirety. Also, try a study Bible focused on the ancient context; it will help illuminate the text.

Knowing the Issues at Stake When Serving the Impoverished

Lupton, Robert D. *Toxic Charity: How Churches and Charities Hurt Those They Help (And How to Reverse It)*. New York: HarperOne, 2011.

Novogratz, Jacqueline. *The Blue Sweater: Bridging the Gap Between Rich and Poor in an Interconnected World*. New York: Rodale Books, 2009.

Sachs, Jeffrey. *The End of Poverty: Economic Possibilities for Our Time*. New York: Penguin Books, 2005.

Understanding Local and Global Poverty Firsthand

Adeney, Miriam. *Kingdom Without Borders: The Untold Story of Global Christianity*. Downers Grove, IL: InterVarsity Press, 2009.

Hall, Ron, and Denver Moore, with Lynn Vincent. *Same Kind of Different as Me*. Nashville: Thomas Nelson, 2006.

Kidder, Tracy. *Mountains Beyond Mountains: The Quest of Dr. Paul Farmer, a Man Who Would Cure the World*. New York: Random House, 2003.

Saada, Tass, with Dean Merrill. *Once an Arafat Man: The True Story of How a PLO Sniper Found a New Life*. Carol Stream, IL: Tyndale, 2010.

What It Means to Be Christian, Church Planting, and Living on Jesus' Mission

Frost, Michael, and Alan Hirsch. *The Shaping of Things to Come: Innovation and Mission for the 21st-Century Church*. Peabody, MA: Hendrickson, 2003.

Goheen, Michael W. *Introducing Christian Mission Today: Scripture, History, and Issues*. Downers Grove, IL: InterVarsity Press, 2014.

Lewis, C. S. *Mere Christianity*. Rev. and ampl. ed. San Francisco, CA: HarperSanFrancisco, 2001.

McNeal, Reggie. *Missional Renaissance: Changing the Scorecard for the Church*. San Francisco: Jossey-Bass, 2009.

Newbigin, Lesslie. *A Word in Season: Perspectives on Christian World Missions*. Grand Rapids, MI: Eerdmans, 1994.

Payne, J. D., *Discovering Church Planting: An Introduction to the Whats, Whys, and Hows of Global Church Planting*. Colorado Springs, CO: Authentic Publishing, 2009.

Wilberforce, William. *A Practical View of Christianity*. Hendrickson Christian Classics. Peabody, MA: Hendrickson, 1996, 2011.

Other Books Well Worth Reading

If you finish that first reading list and want to go even deeper into this subject, here are other resources I've consulted while writing *Jesus' Economy*.

Perspectives on Poverty, Power, Culture, and Justice

Agang, Sunday Bobai. *When Evil Strikes: Faith and the Politics of Human Hostility*. African Christian Studies Series (Book 10). Eugene, OR: Pickwick Publishers, 2016.

Bradley, Anne, and Art Lindsley, eds. *For the Least of These: A Biblical Answer to Poverty*. Grand Rapids, MI: Zondervan, 2015.

Collier, Paul. *The Bottom Billion: Why the Poorest Countries Are Failing and What Can Be Done About It*. Oxford: Oxford University Press, 2007.

Corbett, Steve, and Brian Fikkert. *When Helping Hurts: How to Alleviate Poverty without Hurting the Poor...and Yourself*. Chicago: Moody Publishers, 2014.

Easterly, William. *The White Man's Burden: Why the West's Efforts to Aid the Rest Have Done So Much Ill and So Little Good*. New York: Penguin Press, 2006.

Elmer, Duane. *Cross-Cultural Conflict: Building Relationships for Effective Ministry*. Downers Grove, IL: IVP Academic, 1994.

King, Jr., Martin Luther, *Why We Can't Wait*. Boston: Beacon Press, 1964.

————. *The Measure of a Man*. Philadelphia: The Christian Education Press, 1958.

Lim, Eng Hoe. *The Gospel of the Kingdom: Revealing the Heart of God*. Self-published via CreateSpace, 2012.

Lupton, Robert D. *Compassion, Justice, and the Christian Life: Rethinking Ministry to the Poor*. Ventura, CA: Regal, 2011.

Miller, Michael Matheson, dir. *Poverty Cure*. Grand Rapids, MI: PovertyCure, 2016. DVD.

————, dir. *Poverty, Inc*. Grand Rapids, MI: Passion River Films, 2014. DVD.

Rah, Soong-Chan. *The Next Evangelicalism: Releasing the Church from Western Cultural Captivity*. Downers Grove, IL: InterVarsity Press, 2009.

Richards, E. Randolph, and Brandon J. O'Brien. *Misreading Scripture with Western Eyes: Removing Cultural Blinders to Better Understand the Bible*. Downers Grove, IL: InterVarsity Press, 2012.

Perspectives on Missions

Conn, Harvie M., and Manuel Ortiz. *Urban Ministry: The Kingdom, the City, and the People of God*. Downers Grove, IL: IVP Academic, 2010.

Hirsch, Alan. *The Forgotten Ways: Reactivating the Missional Church*. Grand Rapids, MI: Brazos, 2006.

Newbigin, Lesslie. *The Gospel in a Pluralistic Society*. Grand Rapids, MI: Eerdmans, 1989.

Padilla, C. René. *Mission Between the Times: Essays on the Kingdom*. Grand Rapids, MI: Eerdmans, 1985.

Perspectives on Life Change, Balance, Calling, and Work

Babauta, Leo. *The Power of Less: The Fine Art of Limiting Yourself to the Essential…in Business and in Life*. New York: Hyperion, 2009.

Dayton, Edward R., and Ted W. Engstrom. *Strategy for Living: How to Make the Best Use of Your Time and Abilities*. Ventura, CA: Regal, 1978.

Miller, Donald. *Searching for God Knows What*. Nashville: Thomas Nelson, 2010.

Pemberton, Ryan J. *Called: My Journey to C. S. Lewis's House and Back Again*. Abilene, TX: Leafwood Publishers, 2015.

Swenson, M.D., Richard A. *Margin: Restoring Emotional, Physical, Financial, and Time Reserves to Overloaded Lives*. Colorado Springs, CO: NavPress, 2004.

Whelchel, Hugh. *How Then Should We Work?: Rediscovering the Biblical Doctrine of Work*. Nashville: Westbow Press, 2012.

Perspectives on Entrepreneurship and Business

Berkun, Scott. *The Myths of Innovation*. Sebastopol, CA: O'Reilly Media, 2010.

Godin, Seth. *Linchpin: Are You Indispensable?* New York: Portfolio, 2010.

Lewis, Michael. *Moneyball: The Art of Winning an Unfair Game*. New York: W. W. Norton & Company, 2004.

————. *The Big Short: Inside the Doomsday Machine*. New York: W. W. Norton & Company, 2010.

Osterwalder, Alexander, and Yves Pigneur. *Business Model Generation: A Handbook for Visionaries, Game Changers, and Challengers*. Hoboken, NJ: John Wiley and Sons, 2010.

Stiles, T. J. *The First Tycoon: The Epic Life of Cornelius Vanderbilt*. New York: Knopf, 2009.

ABOUT THE AUTHOR

John D. Barry is a nonprofit CEO, Bible scholar, and pastor. After a career in Christian publishing and Bible software, John and his wife, Kalene, sold their house and nearly everything they owned to dedicate their lives to spreading the gospel and empowering the impoverished. They serve with Jesus' Economy, an innovative nonprofit creating jobs and churches in the developing world. John and Kalene also serve as missionaries with Resurrect Church Movement, the domestic division of Jesus' Economy, equipping U.S. churches to effectively alleviate poverty and bring people to Jesus. John is the general editor of the highly acclaimed *Faithlife Study Bible* and *Lexham Bible Dictionary*, which are used by over one million people, and the author or editor of thirty books, including the popular daily devotional *Connect the Testaments* and the multimedia *DIY Bible Study*. John formerly served as founding publisher of Lexham Press, an imprint of Faithlife Corporation / Logos Bible Software, and as the editor-in-chief of *Bible Study Magazine*, a product he launched.

In a primarily unchurched area of the U.S., John has worked extensively with the homeless, helped plant a church, and started a ministry. Internationally, John has initiated indigenous church planting efforts and the drilling of water wells, and founded an online fair trade marketplace (to empower the impoverished). He is a pastor in the Pacific Northwest and speaks internationally on engaging the Bible, poverty, and spreading the gospel.

To book John for a speaking engagement
or to offer feedback on this book,
email john@jesuseconomy.org.

Connect with John at JesusEconomy.org/John

Make the world a better place.

Jesus' Economy is an innovative 501(c)(3) nonprofit
creating jobs and churches in the developing world.
100% of your donation goes to the cause you choose, every time.

On JesusEconomy.org, you can shop and give to help.

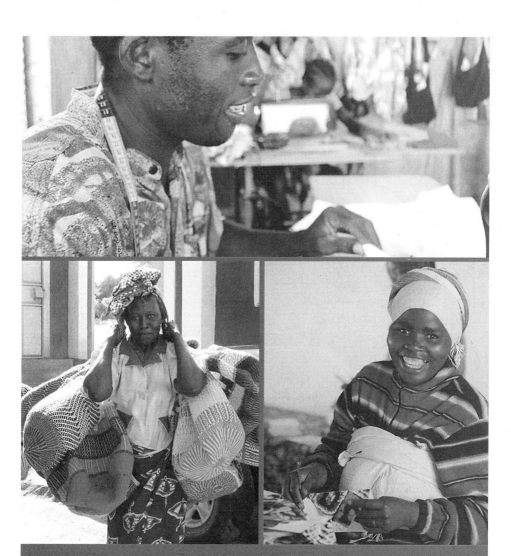

Envision a world where …

Entrepreneurs from developing economies are connected to commerce.
The gospel reaches all people. Basic needs are met everywhere.
The developing world is renewed. That's Jesus' Economy.

JESUS'
ECONOMY

Creating jobs and churches

JesusEconomy.org | 1-855-355-3266